Words to Lift by

Blessing Talk

God bless you,
Teresa

Words To Lift By

Teresa Daniels
with
Blessing Talk

*Conquering Barriers to
Successful Interactions*

Manna House Publishing

Library of Congress Control Number: 2002104328
ISBN: 0-9719282-0-7

Teresa Daniels can be contacted at TeresaDanielsMinistry@hotmail.com
3502 W. Magill Avenue, Fresno, CA 93711-0813

Endorsements

Instinctively, we all crave to be blessed by God and others. And we yearn to give the right kind of blessing to others in appropriate and effective ways. Teresa's wonderful book will enable and empower you to understand the concept of the blessing and to give it to others so that God can use your words to change and enhance lives. After you read her touching stories and biblical, practical ideas, you will have the confidence to know you can be an instrument of blessing in your family and friend's lives.

Kathy Collard Miller, speaker and author of *Why Do I Put So Much Pressure On Myself?*

Men desire to make an impact in their family and friend's lives but often their stoic and "just do it" perspective of life makes it difficult for them to touch others emotionally. *Words to Lift By* by Teresa Daniels will be of particular interest to men because it gives them understanding about the necessity of blessing others, and even more important, enables them with practical ideas for reaching out to others in God's chosen way.

Larry Miller, speaker and author of *What's in the Bible for Couples?*

Teresa Daniels has done an excellent job in recognizing that we all long to be blessed by God as well as others. Her book, *Words to Lift By* will help you realize the significance of blessing others and equip you with practical tools to do so in a way that honors God and those to be blessed. It's a must read for Christian leaders.

Gerry Wakeland, Former Director of Women's Ministries, Crystal Cathedral, Garden Grove, California

It is exciting to see this book in print! People are changed as Biblical blessings are received and given, and this book offers insight and instruction on making this a part of your life. Over the years I've watched Teresa live and teach the principles of *Words to Lift By, Blessing Talk*. I highly recommend it.

Shirley Barber, Minister for Women, Peoples Church, Fresno, California

Teresa Daniels writes and teaches principles from the Word of God, on which her life is based – principles she has passed on to her family, her friends, and audiences across the country. I highly recommend Words to Lift By, Blessing Talk for anyone who is looking for a way in which to encourage another through the words they speak.

Pat Clary
Author, Speaker

Acknowledgments

The original core of the material for *Words to Lift By* was developed for Women's Ministries Institute under the direction of Pat Clary. Thanks, Pat, for the opportunities and encouragement.

This book came into existence because of the kind badgering of my husband, Noel. His love, encouragement support, and assistance are treasures I don't take for granted. He blesses me!

My heartfelt thanks go to my daughter, Sara Candelaria, for her cheerful and insightful editing, to Pam Farrel and Tyler Daniels for constructive and thoughtful suggestions, and Ginger Niemeyer.

VIII

For Noel,
My best friend and true partner,
biggest supporter and love of my life,
who taught me how to snuggle in the struggle.

X

TABLE OF CONTENTS

FORWARD

Even as I write, the nation is waiting to hear the jury's decision relative to the guilt or innocence of a mother who drowned her five children. She seemingly did this terrible thing out of mental and physical stress that simply was more than she could handle. What a shame she did not have this book in her hand, or that someone was not able to apply its principles to *her*. It is a message of guidance and encouragement at a time when so many are needing a word of hope in what often seems to be a hopeless world.

It is a pleasure to whole heartedly commend this book to you, which I believe will be a word from the Lord, lifting you to a higher plane as you read it, and others as you put it into practice.

Rev. G. L. Johnson
Senior Pastor
Peoples Church
Fresno, California

INTRODUCTION

"No, you can't help me."

She had walked through the door hesitantly, looking reluctant and guarded. Her expression, what there was of it, had revealed little. While others moved on around her chatting and laughing, she'd slowly walked part way through the foyer where her progress stalled. One of the chatting throng nearly tripped over the newcomer, said "Excuse me," and kept going.

When one more observant and sensitive soul had paused to ask if she could help, the newcomer had shaken her head as she'd turned her down and just hurried toward an open seat. She had, of course, heard the "Are you sure?" called after her, but she didn't answer. A connection had been attempted, but none was made.

Without a little probing, it's impossible to say just what *blocked that interaction, but there certainly was an unseen obstacle of some sort!*

I imagine you assumed this interaction happened in the foyer of a church, but it could have as easily taken place at a PTA meeting or near the entrance of a large business. But let's suppose for a moment it *was* in a church. It could also just as easily have gone this way:

"Hello! I'm Teresa Daniels, and you're . . .? "Janice Roper? I'm so glad to meet you, Janice. Is this your first visit to our church? Welcome! I know this church looks huge on your first visit, but really we're the largest small church in town. People are what count most with us. You'll find there are friends and activities that will particularly interest you and address any needs you might have."

Reaching out to *lightly* hold on to Janice's arm while attention shifts to a women near-by, "Hi, Sue. I'd like you to meet Janice Roper. This is her first time here. Are you going on in to the service? I need to get back to the choir room; May Janice go in with you? It's always nice to have someone to sit with. Thanks! While you wait for things to get started, perhaps you could tell her a little about some of the programs we have here. Great." Giving Sue a quick hug, I add, "You're the best, Sue. I knew I could count on you. Janice is going to love you as much as I do! Feel free to ask a favor of me next time!"

Then turning back to Janice I say, "Janice, you really are going to like Sue. She's a sweetheart. And I know if you're anything like me you're going to love this church. I'm looking forward to seeing you again!"

In these very brief interactions, I gave *two* blessings and opened the door of welcome so wide Janice would be hard pressed not to feel special, warmed and accepted. Wouldn't you?

Speaking words that aren't blocked by unseen obstacles is the least of my little grandson's problems right now, but it's a formidable challenge for the rest of us. As my daughter, Sara, pointed out recently, "It's so much fun now that Joel is learning to talk!" We're starting to have real interactions with him and some of our attempts at communication are beginning to connect! He's trying to form and use real words, which is a wonderful beginning, but

16

he has a *lot* of words to learn yet. He'll have the same challenge (like each of us did) of learning which words to actually say, when and how to say them, and then he'll still have to deal with those barriers to interaction! *This is a life-long process* we could all use some help with!

As human beings, our foremost method of contact with others is talking, and as believers, every contact we have is **an opportunity for active partnering with God!** Each of those contacts brings with it the potential to lift up, support, and build other people. The problem is each contact also brings with it two other possibilities. We can have no effect at all, or we can actually tear down and do harm! The meaning of Christian is 'one who is like Christ.' In our imitation of Jesus and His work, He calls us into relationship to one another as He is in relationship with us. He makes a place for us in His body so we can be connected to other believers, and then within that relational framework, He calls us all to active partnering with Him. Inevitably, it involves dealing with and reaching out *to people.* Of course, that's no big surprise, but do you realize that even the *simplest contacts* have a relational aspect? Whether it is a behind the scenes service like washing dishes after a potluck, a front-line task like teaching a Sunday school class, interacting with people on our job, or a parent talking to his child at home, how we interact with people is critical.

In leadership or not, none of us set out to be ineffective in our interactions with others. Yet all too often our efforts to "reach out and touch someone" *don't connect!* You send, but they do not receive; it's as if an obstacle blocks the way. Perhaps you have found yourself in that position, aware that there are hindrances of some sort that get in the road of successful interactions. I know I have. My story about the woman in the foyer was fictional, but I've seen lots of real incidents like it.

With a background of communication (my degree is in speech), I can't help observing and analyzing interactions. People have both verbal and non-verbal 'talk,' and I've been in a position to observe *lots* of interactions between people that didn't connect. I've been a Bible teacher and a leader in women's ministry for over thirty-five years, the last twenty-eight at Peoples Church in Fresno, California (a church of five thousand.) I've also been a teacher and trainer for small group facilitating, a seminar and retreat speaker, as well as a vice president / teaching associate for Women's Ministries Institute for nearly half that time. Sadly, I can't begin to count the failed interactions I've observed.

When connection fails, the door is opened for so many things to go awry. It's at such points that discouragement for a child can begin or rebellion for a teen. It's so easy for a misunderstanding to come between a husband and wife, between friends or neighbors. Failed interactions can create havoc in the workplace, in committees or on church boards, and it can lie at the root of conflict in a family, a people, or between nations. Failed interactions can grow, becoming more negative and destructive, finally leading to much bigger, more serious results: divorce, the end of friendship, loss of a job, the taking up of arms, the splitting of churches. They can cause people to miss out on God's plan for their lives. There is so much bad that isn't avoided but could have been, and so much good that is missed by verbal and non-verbal connections that are blocked by important things that look small in the beginning.

It reminds me of the nursery rhyme about the missing horseshoe nail[1]:

For want of a nail, the shoe was lost.
For want of a shoe, the horse was lost.
For want of a horse, the rider was lost.
For want o a rider, battle was lost.
For want of a battle, the kingdom was lost.
... And all for the want of a horseshoe nail!

Ah, but what could those hindrances / blocks be? I thought and prayed about what I observed and I realized it was possible to identify major blocks to successful interactions. I have found these to be particularly significant and, unfortunately, common.

Low self-esteem
Lacking love and being unnoticed / unappreciated
Loneliness and isolation
Lacking a vision for one's own future
Lack of follow-through and support given to them.

These potential problems can hinder people from receiving the benefits that come from successful interactions with others and prevent them from receiving all God has for them – help which would enable them to develop lives of greater success, satisfaction and effectiveness.

19

There is a format[2] for giving a blessing in the Old Testament that enables Christians to help the people the Lord places in our paths conquer these obstacles using words that lift. The steps of the blessing correlate beautifully to these problems or hindrances.

This book will teach you *how* to use this format to bless, to speak words apt for God's use in personal and public interactions. The steps of the blessing include:

Positive, concrete contact, usually as a physical touch,
Personal affirmation,
Particular language specifically appropriate for the one
        being blessed,
Painting a vision of hope and
Partnering for follow-through.

If you look back at the interchange I had with my fictional friends, Janice and Sue, you'll see the elements of the blessing are all there. None of the steps of this biblical format involve things you can't do as well. I'm sure you have. Any one of them alone is helpful, but used together they produce amazing results. I have taught the concepts in this book in seminars and workshops for a number of years, and the response always overwhelms me. Many have said it changed the way they looked at their interactions with people. They found people warmly respond to being blessed

---

[2]Gary Smalley and John Trent wrote a wonderful book, *The Blessing*, in 1986 in which they brought the Christian world's attention to the biblical format for blessing. Their work laid the foundation to my understanding and had an important impact on the initiation of my study of blessing and its application for ministry interactions.

and that it does indeed open the way for further successful interactions. Over and over I was urged to put this teaching in a book

Let me encourage you, dear friend; God sees your attempts to connect meaningfully with the people He has set before you. He will enable you to do exceedingly abundantly above anything you could ever ask or think. Others have found that following the format of biblical blessing enabled the Lord to powerfully work through them and He will use it to work through you, too!

"A word aptly spoken is like apples of gold in settings of silver." Proverbs 25:11

When you enhance your skill to interact and communicate by incorporating the steps of a biblical blessing into your conversation, you can more effectively relate God's love, your love, and your support to others. You can use it to greatly increase your effectiveness in the interactions the Lord presents for you. You can use this pattern to bless your family and friends. You can implement it in your interactions on your job without ever directly quoting a verse. You can help people realize the Lord has plans for His people, plans to prosper and not to harm, to give hope and a future. Jeremiah 29:11. Giving a blessing encourages and lifts in and of itself, but it also has the potential for ministry on another level. It can extend beyond that immediate interaction to open an avenue for more. It is a wonderful aid for your use in helping people receive what the Lord has for them. The person with obstacles in his life needs our help to get over them. We can do that as we lift them with words of blessing.

"The lips of the righteous nourish many
...the mouth of the righteous is a fountain of life."
Proverbs 10:21a, 10:11a

Words spoken specifically to bless are as precious as gold. I know first hand. At a moment of great need, a blessing which followed the biblical format was given to me and its impact is still blessing me years later. **You** too can be a person who gives powerful biblical blessings and find your words have immediate impact on your interactions for ministry, as well tearing down blocks people have to receiving future ministry.

You can be one who knows
how to offer *Words that truly Lift*...
Blessing talk!

"*A word aptly spoken is like apples of gold in settings of silver.*"

Proverbs 25:11

Part One
The Biblical Blessing

"The lips of the righteous nourish many"

Proverbs 10:21

Chapter One
THE NATURE OF BLESSING

KEY TERMS

Blessing
Invoking or acting as a catalyst for the activation of God's Word and will in the life of another.

Invoking
To cause, bring forth, or bring about.

Activation
Igniting or causing something to begin.

KEY QUESTIONS

- ❖ What are the settings of scriptural blessing?
- ❖ What is the format for scripture based blessing?
- ❖ What is its purpose?
- ❖ What are the steps of biblical blessing?
- ❖ How do the steps of blessing correlate to the identified obstacles?
- ❖ What prompts blessing?

The Definition of Blessing

To see why a blessing is helpful for lifting, it's useful to look at the definition of blessing. Literally it means to kneel before another as a way to acknowledge that person's high value. Usually we visualize a blessing being given opposite of this – the one seeking blessing kneeling before the one who is to give it. This reversal is a very foreign concept to American culture. We went to a great deal of trouble to avoid having anyone we were expected to kneel in front of! Christians understand the concept of exalting God as king and being humble before Him, but kneeling before another *person* is another matter entirely! However, if our goal is to help lift people over the obstacles that impede them, what better way than to bend down to give them a boost? Actually, the definition o blessing is firmly in line with New Testament teaching. Paul directs us not to think of ourselves more highly than we ought, Romans 12:3, but rather in humility consider others better than ourselves. Philippians 2:3

Metaphorically kneeling before the one we would bless also makes good sense from another vantage point. If the one who is blocked from receiving ministry could climb over the obstacles in his way, he probably would have done it already! The person whose way is blocked may realize he struggles, but not be able to identify why exactly. It is the responsibility of the one with the "Good News" to reach out. When the situation is one Christian reaching out to another, again it is the responsibility of the one who is already over the hurdle to aid the one struggling with it. It's a wonderful example of the servant heart Jesus desires for us as we "serve one another in love." Galatians 5:13

Blessing is a means of extending grace or favor. Just as God extends grace to us though we don't merit it, as we offer blessing we pass on the favor which was first given to us.

Perhaps most important of all, blessing is the invoking or activation of God's Word and will in the life of another. Let's break that down and look at it.

First, then idea of **invoking** is usually used in the context of an invocation in our culture. At the beginning of meetings or formal gatherings it's often customary to have a religious dignitary give one. An invocation is essentially a rather formal prayer to a deity (in these politically correct times, usually a very vague one!) to ask for aid, protection, inspiration or the like. However, in the case of a blessing, a secondary definition comes into play. Instead of speaking *to* God, it is a means of speaking words God has given with the earnest desire to cause them to come to pass. It is the *pronouncing or uttering* of what *God says.*

Second, **activation** obviously carries with it the idea of igniting or causing something to begin. In blessing, speaking the words out loud gives them life and power because they are more than just words we dream up ourselves. It is God's Word and will, not our own, that is being invoked and activated. It isn't flattery or fluff, nor is it simply what we

30

wish or hope for. It is based in God's Word, selected and directed by the Holy Spirit.

Finally, blessing is **inspired by the Holy Spirit**. He provides the motivation, enables us to identify the opportunity, supplies the content and phrasing, and gives direction as to when and how a blessing is to be given.

We'll look at each of those concepts more carefully as we go along.

Scripture Based Blessing Overview

The steps of the biblical blessing correspond to the things that block the work of the Holy Spirit in the lives of people who need connection for ministry. These steps need not be extensive or comprehensive, but they are *cumulative* in effect; the more elements included in an interaction there are, the more powerful it becomes.

❖ Blessing interactions begin with a **positive, concrete contact, usually a physical touch.** That may seem somewhat odd, but it is amazing how powerful such a contact can be. It is more than just a gesture toward someone; it is both a definite and usually physical touch that puts the first chink in the wall. It has the power to lift in and of itself. Even the phone company knows that when you reach out and touch someone, that person feels loved and cared about. The same insight is behind the advertising slogan Hallmark greeting cards use, "When you care enough to send the very best." Such a purposeful contact correlates to the block of feeling unloved. It can take the form of laying on of hands or

31

anointing with oil, be as simple as an embrace or a hand shake, or be a contact that is made by phone or mail. Obviously, there are advantages to the contact being made in person, but when that isn't possible, blessing can still be effective. Putting a blessing in writing does have the benefit that it can bless again and again.

❖ **Personal affirmation** usually happens at the same time the touch is extended. It is accomplished by using the person's name, which is an easy way to single him out, emphasizing his inherent value. When we speak directly to someone, giving him our full attention, it affirms the fact that he is in a position of worth to me, and that I accept him. When it takes place in connection to the church, an acceptance in the group is communicated. If the person is an unbeliever, it doesn't mean he is accepted as a member of the family of faith, but the door of welcome and opportunity is clearly opened. Giving affirmation in this way coupled with a purposed contact works to counter low self-esteem and the feelings of being unloved and unnoticed or unappreciated.

❖ **Particular language** that is chosen especially for the one being blessed continues the process. It is inspired by the Holy Spirit as we make ourselves available to Him. Naturally, the Holy Spirit will always give words that are consistent with God's Word. The language of blessing is always spoken positively. They are selected for the one being blessed, and apply directly and primarily to him. The spoken words of a biblical blessing correspond to the block of loneliness and isolation.

❖ **Painting a vision of hope** is a very important part of a blessing. It describes what the Spirit prompts vividly. It gives encouragement, reinforcing the concept of God's wonderful plans for the one being blessed, thereby providing hope. Envisioning a future especially focused for a person in a blessing correlates to the lack of vision and hopelessness block.

❖ **Partnering for follow-through** must be active and real in blessing. It's actually a three-way partnering, because as you commit to support in some way or to uphold him in prayer, you are also partnering with God in what He desires to do for and with him. It is a commitment to encourage, love, and remind the person of how valuable he is and what God is doing for him. This active partnering for follow-through correlates with the longing for support and commitment that can block ministry.

As you may have noticed by now, the elements of the biblical blessing have an overlapping aspect in addressing the problem, need areas. As a consequence, the more elements that are included in an expression of blessing, the more powerful it becomes. So, where does the pattern for blessing come from?

"Therefore encourage one another and build each other up, just as in fact you are doing."

1 Thessalonians 5:11

Chapter Two
BLOCKS TO INTERACTION

KEY TERMS

Interaction
Action or influence that is between, mutual, reciprocal

Self-esteem
Self-respect; self-view; self-valuation.

Isolation
To be set or placed apart, detached or separated so as to be alone.

KEY QUESTIONS

❖ What is the need for blessing?
❖ What are common problems that block successful interactions?
❖ How is low self-esteem manifested in our culture?
❖ In what ways is loneliness a problem?
❖ How is hope related to having a vision for the future?
❖ Why is partnering for support important?

Blessing to the Rescue

Have you ever been really low & needed lifting? I mean *really* low – so low, as comedians have put it, you have to look up to see your shoe laces? I have. It came as quite a surprise to me as a young woman who was raised in a very happy Christian home, was married to her very best friend and had two darling little children. I thought my life was picture perfect.

In the seventh grade I read an article by Ruth Bell Graham in which she wrote of a practice she began when she was a little girl in China with her missionary parents. She explained how she started praying each day for the man she would marry – that God would teach, guide, and protect him. I remember thinking, "Wow, what a great idea; she ended up with Billy Graham!" I decided to do the same. I didn't know it yet, but I had already met the one I was praying for.

Noel Daniels' family had just moved to my Southern California community. His dad was the new pastor of a thriving church in town. When we got into high school we had classes together and became good friends. Right from the start we had a lot in common: classes, friends, and especially our faith. We had a particularly important thing in common as well. We both understood that it was essential to seek the Lord about who we should date and marry. We each did that as we dated on and off over time. When we did marry toward the end of college there wasn't any doubt God had arranged the whole thing. That awareness became very important seven years later.

When Lisa, our second child, was 3 years old she was diagnosed with a non-treatable genetic disorder that resulted from Noel and I both having a <u>very</u> rare recessive gene. If only one of us had had it, it would not have become operative. The doctors told us they didn't really know too much about mucopolysacaridosis – it was so rare many of the staff at Los Angeles Children's Hospital had never actually seen a case. They thought there would probably be some dwarfing and other physical abnormalities, but they were sure it would cause her to be developmentally delayed. The prognosis was left purposefully vague, but they expected she would eventually attain about a six-year development level with a thirty-year life-expectancy. It was very similar to the prognosis we would have been given if it had been Down's Syndrome. Though that sounds awful, it actually sounds better than reality turned out to be. At 3 she was a bit behind; during the next months she rapidly began to regress instead of progress slowly, as the doctors predicted. It was bad news to start with, and it just got worse.

Each day that first year was hard, but some days were impossibly hard. I cried every day, though even Noel didn't know how much of a struggle some of those days were for me. Like the day Lisa dumped out a little vase of straw flowers for the *third* time in a single morning. They were tiny little brittle things that made a tangled mess to pick up. I collapsed in a sobbing heap on my bedroom floor, totally overwhelmed. It was the proverbial straw that broke the camel's back. Lisa stood watching me with her huge blue eyes, thumb in mouth, brow furrowed in confusion. She turned her back to me,

38

plopped down in my lap and lifted her little hand over her shoulder ...to softly pat my cheek. I carry the memory of that sweet moment like a picture in a locket made of flesh.

There weren't many more sweet moments like that one, though. She was rapidly disappearing before our very eyes. More and more she was like a precious dwelling where the resident wasn't always home. It was hard, and it just kept getting harder. I remember one day in particular. The news the doctor gave me that day wasn't any worse than the others in the long string of bad reports. Perhaps it was just that the string was one report too long, like straw flowers dumped out for the third time. I can't tell you why I was devastated *that* day. I just was. My sister-in-law called and asked me to go for donuts, coffee & sisterly catching up. It was always a special time when we went to coffee and I thought of it as great treat, but that day I just wanted to sit in the dark somewhere. I didn't even have the emotional strength left to say no.

So I went ... reluctantly.

She realized immediately what a mess I was. We took our coffee outside and talked as we walked in sunshine that I didn't notice. She patiently listened as I poured out my grief and pain. Often during those days the Lord had ministered to me through His Word, but now it seemed like something was in the way. I told her I knew God could heal; I had seen it. I had been searching the Scriptures, claiming verses, fervently praying for Lisa's healing, believing for it with all my might, but my well of faith had run dry. I couldn't believe for healing or anything else. Like I said, I was so low that I had to look up to see my shoelaces. She listened between the lines as we sipped and strolled, then lovingly put her arm through mine, drawing me close as we walked. Neither of us knew anything about a biblical blessing, but the Lord knew exactly

39

what I needed. Because she highly valued me, she dropped everything to comfort me. It was as if the world stopped for the time we were together. She offered me words of encouragement when I desperately needed them. She said, "Teresa, it's all right to feel bad. I understand. God gave us to each other for times like this."

Just her empathy was a comfort, but she didn't stop there. She painted the vision of a special future for me. "I know you can't believe God is at work in this right now. That's OK. He's still working things for your good, making a way for you, even when you can't see." Then she gave me the best gift I had ever received. She said, "Lean on me for now ... I'll believe for you."

The biblical blessing Joan gave me contained all of the steps that make a blessing based on the Bible's format so powerful and effective. And it was *powerfully effective* in both encouraging and lifting me over the obstacles I couldn't overcome on my own. What she said were truly words to lift by; her blessing lifted me when my spiritual and emotional strength was all gone.

The Need for Blessing

Why do you need to know how to incorporate blessing language into your interactions with people?
There is a great need for it!

There are people all around us that need lifting more than we can possibly see on the surface. They put on their public or their church " I'm fine, how are you?" persona, and too often we take them at face value. In answer to "How are you?" I often replied, "fine" when I didn't feel fine at all! Those who didn't try to look behind my mask never knew different. Lots of loving folks had the opportunity to bless me but never perceived the need. Thankfully, I had the encouraging blessings of dear ones like Joan, the unfaltering support of Noel, and God's grace to help me finally come out of the tunnel of that first year. Eleven years later the Lord took Lisa home, but blessing and grace had opened the door for 'joy to come in the morning' long before.

Obviously, we realize people have issues and problems that need ministry - that's a big part of why they come to church. It's the same reason God brings them across our paths beyond the church doors in places like the donut shop! Even when we're not looking to meet someone, the Lord places them before us in spots like the grocery store, and gives us eyes to see them if we will only look up from our shopping carts! We really want the Lord reach and touch people, and we know He wants to do it through us. It begins to happen when we open our eyes and hearts to the need. But, like others with hindrances blocking their way, I couldn't seem to get beyond them without help. It was like a think, brick wall with no visible door to knock on!

As I considered my own experience, I realized that feeling alone and lacking vision were the obstacles I struggled with when Joan broke through my sense of isolation and its dead end to connect with me. When Noel was gone to work I felt very alone, and I couldn't picture a future that I thought was actually possible for my little family. I thought about these blocks and the others I had identified and considered how blessing addressed them. The question

41

naturally presented itself, "How can I incorporate the steps of biblical blessing into my communications with the people *I am called to reach* in a way that the Lord can use to meet those needs and free them to receive all He has for them through me? The exciting things I discovered as I studied and experimented is what I'm going to share with you in this book.

Let's take a closer look at these potential blocks to see why they create such problems and opportunities for us. The first two, low self-esteem and feeling unloved and unnoticed or unappreciated strongly overlap, so I'm going to deal with them together.

❖ **Low self-esteem** and **being unloved and unnoticed or unappreciated** go hand in hand. In fact, I would content that low-self esteem is the logical consequence of being unloved and/or unnoticed.

I realize the secular world is making a lot of the issue of self-esteem, especially in education. I am aware of Christians who reject it as a legitimate problem because of a perception that the secular solution is a glorification of self and selfishness, but a real obstacle has been identified here and we dare not ignore it just because those outside the church can see it, too.

No one wakes up one day and decides to have a low opinion of himself. He has to be carefully taught by words and actions or neglect. Everyone wants to be reached out to in love, but that's exactly what some don't experience. There is a deep human need to feel special, worthwhile, and valuable, but some don't receive purposeful, concrete / physical contact or verbal feedback that's affirms their basic worth. A person's self opinion can't help but reflect

42

the perceived opinions of others, especially those of the significant people in his life ~ parents, grandparents, teachers. People come to believe things like 'I'm no good,' 'I'm stupid,' 'I'm a loser' or 'I don't deserve better' based on what people and experience have told them. The number of stars, presidents, professional athletes and a myriad of other things is limited. Kids learn early that only a select few will win most of the honors. If they're not made to feel special or they don't find a way to shine, it's a short step to feeling less important or less valuable than other people. Albert Einstein was certainly one of those who was counted a superstar in his own field. However, he believed stars shouldn't be considered more important than other people. He once said, "It strikes me as unfair, and even in bad taste, to select a few individuals for boundless admiration, attributing superhuman powers of mind and character to them.[3]

Our culture usually saves its praise for the noteworthy among us. Unfortunately, for every winner there are a lot of losers. How many times have you seen someone win something and remark, "Wow! I never win anything!" I've heard that line lots of times at everything from parties with games to the food prize winner at a fast food restaurant.

Likewise, not feeling special or worthy of being singled out (a winner) can be true for people even in churches, and the bigger the church, the more likely it is. We tend to praise the leader by name and mostly ignore the contributions of the "little" people, that is if any accolades are given out at all. We know as believers that we don't work for the Lord for the accolades, but it is difficult to continue ministering over time if we begin to feel that what we contribute makes no difference and is so insignificant that no one knows, notices or cares what we do. We are called to be part of a body, and while some parts are more obvious, all are important.

None the less, there are going to be just so many who are "up front," and while the rest of us will be important we won't be stars. Most of us can tolerate being a rather average worker bee if we were (and are) made to feel special at home. But what about all of those who were never good enough at home either? I read once that it takes fourteen positive comments to counteract a negative one. The number stuck in my memory, perhaps because it was so big. I don't know about you, but the negative comments I receive really stick out to me! Even if a person is complimented now and then, it's my experience that criticism easily outweighs those comments. There's probably a definitive study somewhere, but I'm inclined to think that a ratio 14 to 1 is on the right track. How catastrophic then that criticism has been a constant in the lives of many and praise a rarity. I have talked to a number of people who can't remember *ever* being praised at home while they were growing up but they can *vividly* remember being criticized! While there may be a little selective memory involved for some, it's a certainty there was far more criticism than praise. The sure result of that kind of experience is low self-esteem. Smalley and Trent addressed this issue at length in *The Blessing*, and contended that *many* people didn't receive the approval and acceptance -the blessing- of their parents, citing example after example. After my own conversations with people over years of ministry, I can't help but agree.

It's possible to feel accepted, approved and loved by a mom (or other significant person) but believe her opinion of your worth is biased and thus not really true. In that case you can feel loved and have really low self-esteem anyway. That was true of me in junior high school, and was probably true for a lot of you as well, but it was temporary. However, low self-esteem and feeling unloved or unnoticed are usually a permanent duo.

We live in an amazingly selfish era. Being self focused is encouraged in our culture to the point of overlooking those around us who need and deserve our attention. "I've got to be me," "I did it my way," and "I deserve to be happy" are mottos of our age. People who grew up in homes from the time they were small where their parents were busy 'being all they could be' or chasing the 'American dream' (i. e. the big house, new car, etc.) bear emotional scars from the lack of connection they felt. I suspect that the kid who buys the explanation "I'm doing this all for you" is rare indeed! *

Children whose parents divorce are another group of kids who have a lot of potential for feeling greatly unloved

---

*This is not the situation for parents who are struggling just trying to make ends meet, of course. The bigger and better versions of the American dream and self-fulfillment don't come into play when the primary driving force is keeping your head above water! Putting their child in day-care is the only option for many, but even when conscientious parents select the best care possible, it doesn't mean the child might not *feel* abandoned. Believers have a great advantage in this situation because God is so gracious to step in and fill gaps for us, and a biblical blessing is a tool God can really use to *protect* a child's sense of self-worth.

and unconnected. Please take note that it isn't that they feel like *they're the only ones* in their situation; half or more of their friend's are probably from broken homes as well. Only a generation ago, the child whose parents divorced was stigmatized by virtue of the fact that it was looked down on by society and rare. Not so today. On the contrary, the child whose parents have not divorced and each spouse only married once are in the minority. Our son, Tyler, was shocked to discover that his two-parent, non-divorced, happy (most of the time!) family was quite unusual at the *Christian* college he attended!

To separate because of physical or emotional abuse can be a genuine necessity. There are lots of folks who didn't want a divorce but were handed one, anyway. In addition, more and more single women and men who didn't understand what their poor choices were going to cost them are raising children by themselves. A single, dedicated parent can raise children who feel loved and accepted; it may be hard, but it's certainly possible with the Lord, particularly with the loving help of family, friends, and the church.

Such single parent situations having been acknowledged, there are still *lots* of kids who end up in single parent homes because of divorces in which couples take a way out of a difficult situation that discounts how hard the break-up of the family really is on kids. Over and over I've had people tell me they *felt* rejected by the parent who moved out, even while acknowledging that it probably wasn't the case! Worse, even years later some comment how they still feel torn by divided loyalties and lingering suspicions that it was somehow their fault. The idea that the child 'will get over' it is often overly optimistic. He'll adjust, but my experience is that for most, lingering pain and bitterness from feeling unloved or abandoned is just under the surface.

In addition, there is large group of kids who feel unloved because of overt rejection. We've all seen documentaries on the young people on the streets of our big cities. Many of them explain that they were kicked out by their parent(s) or whoever was raising them. Called 'throw-away kids' by those who reach out to them, they are there because their parents couldn't or wouldn't deal with them anymore. They are, in short, unwanted.

While other kids on the street no doubt run away from loving homes because of rebellion against parents perceived as unfair or too strict, far too many are fleeing abuse. Abuse clearly equals not being loved.

Kids aren't the only ones who feel unloved and abandoned. Divorce takes a terrible toll not just on children, but on the spouse who is rejected. Among the worst words in the world have got to be these: "I don't love you anymore."

Add to the ignored, abused, and abandoned all those who are in a job, an organization or a church whose work goes unappreciated or unacknowledged, and you end up with a *huge* number of people feeling unloved and unappreciated.

❖ **Loneliness and isolation** are also major problems. Most of us have felt isolated or lonely at one time or another, but for some it is a constant in their lives. It can particularly be true for single people, the divorced, and the widowed. Our culture's activities are often set up for couples. Thankfully, the Church is working hard to have programs for singles and this is helping, but it is still a big problem.

I had a wonderful and supportive husband during the horrible first year of learning to cope with Lisa's condition, but he had the respite of a job outside the home. For me, handling the role of primary care-giver became an increasingly great challenge which often made me feel isolated and lonely. Children who become primary care-givers for elderly parents can end up in the same position.

I've talked to many young, stay-at-home moms who feel quite isolated and lonely, too. Though they love their little ones and want to care for them themselves, the day can seem endlessly long with only small children around. Soap operas and daytime television take up time, but certainly won't fill the void, in fact they might make it worse. All too often, when their husbands get home and they finally have a grown-up to talk to, they find a tired man who is all talked out. Talking with his wife is frequently the last thing he wants to do!

The very successful can be extremely lonely, as well. Ever hear the expression, "It's lonely at the top?" Noel pointed out to me that many who are successful find that others treat them differently. This can be true for business executives, sports and media stars, pastors of large churches, heads of organizations, as well as the very wealthy. A company's top salesman may be ensuring everyone else is able to keep their jobs, but not be asked to play on the company bowling team! It's a mistake to assume a person who "has it made" doesn't need the lifting a blessing can give them!

People who are unusual in some way are very likely to make this list, too. People with disabilities or addictions, the unlovely or unsuccessful, the abused or socially inept (among others) can end up on the fringe of society, isolated and lonely.

A new film from Denmark was reviewed on the radio recently by Los Angeles Times film critic Kenneth Turan called *Italian for Beginners*.[4]   One line was quoted that obviously struck a chord with the reviewer as it had with the characters in the film. It was uttered by a pastor. "It is in loneliness that God seems farthest away."

❖ **Lacking a vision for one's own future** is a challenge that's not quite so obvious. Considering the fact that lots of people are avidly pursuing careers and success, it's amazing how many don't have a clear vision for their future. In fact, an amazing number of people I have asked don't have much of an answer to questions regarding their future at all. Questions like, "Where do you see yourself five years from now?" or "What do you hope to accomplish this year?" often prompt a response of "I don't know." As Jackie, a stressed working mom puts it, "I'm running in circles, never getting anywhere. Actually, considering my carpooling, that would be 'driving' in circles!" A frustrated clerk remarked to me that the faster he works, the 'behinder' he gets.

Hope is the natural result of having a personal vision for the future, and my observation is that hope is in rather short supply in our world. Even when an individual faces his need for hope and realizes he has very little, it's not the sort of thing one can simply decide to get! It's not like you can go to the store and buy some. Hope comes from having a vision of your future that is *positive and possible*. The person who has never been told he will succeed isn't likely to have a positive vision for his future. How much more the one who has been told he is no good, he is stupid, or he'll never amount to anything! I've come across people who grew up in homes like that, haven't you? Perhaps it sounds like your own.

❖ **Many lack any committed partnering for support follow-through.** This basic human need is required for our very survival in our earliest days, and while we outgrow the need for direct, intensive parental care, we don't outgrow our need for the committed connection. We never outgrow our desire for parental support and approval. We may not need physical or financial support from our parents, but support by encouragement, praise and approval can be just as strategic.

The value of the commitment of friends can't be over emphasized, either. The television series 'Seinfeld' was often referred to as a show about nothing, but that's not really true. It was a show about friendship (apparently even shallow people feel the need for friends who are there for them!) The show 'Friends' is even more direct about the value of 'I'm there for you.' Committed friends can be a source of comedy, but more important, they are a source of stability and strength.

For generations songs have expressed this need in phrases like 'love you forever,' 'always be true,' and 'I will always be there.' One of the greatest hurts a person can experience is the sense of betrayal that comes from the breach of commitment in adultery. Those who haven't even made that much of a commitment still speak in terms like 'my girlfriend (boyfriend) was cheating on me.'

God never intended for us to be alone and commitment is an integral part of that. Obviously we can't partner for follow-through with everyone who might need it, but we can pass on what the Lord has given to us as He directs and gives opportunity.

The Lord leads people across our paths that *really need* blessing. Often they have one or more of these blocks to connecting with us and receiving the very things they need by ministry from the Lord through us. The person who is called to minister has the obligation to breech the wall, not the person who is trapped behind it!

While there are possibilities for blessing all around us, our greatest opportunities are going to be in our churches. Those who make the effort to actually get to a church are much more likely to open to the Lord's overtures, including the ones that come through you! Henry Blackaby, author of *Experiencing God,*[5] made the point that leaders have stewardship responsibility for their people. Shepherds must look out for the flock. But, how can a single pastor or leader look out for a whole flock and still head up the programs, do the preaching, or whatever else his role may entail?

Since we know that even those of us who are not in leadership at a given moment are called to ministry, we can't leave all the ministry work to just a few. It won't all get done. It can't. What's more, God intended it that way. From the beginning, God purposed that all His people be a part of the work He wanted done in this world. Through Moses He called us to be a kingdom of priests, Exodus 19:6, and through Peter, a royal priesthood (1 Peter 2:5.) We each play a part in the functioning of the body. You may not be a primary shepherd, a pastor, woman's ministry director, or even officially a leader, but *you are a minister*. We all have people the Lord wants *us* to take note of and help with. When we reach and bless another, we in turn will be blessed. It's the Matthew 6:33 principle: when we seek the kingdom first, working as His instrument, everything else we need comes to us. Anyone can be used by God to bless. I really believe you end up getting what you give. You want to be blessed? Give blessing.

Folks who come to our churches and receive the ministry they need stick around. But have you noticed how many people have been part of your fellowship and are gone now? Does your church have a directory that was made a few years ago? Take a look. If your church is like most, the only missing people won't be just those who have gone home to be with the Lord. Oh, sure, you'll have some kids who grew up and landed somewhere else after they graduated from school, as well as the ones whose companies relocated them, but what about the others? Where are those people who you still see from time to time but aren't in church anymore?

We work hard to seek the lost sheep. So why aren't we more concerned with watching over them, tending them, once they come near? Who is going to be eager to leave a flock where they are loved, fed, cared for? Where they can get to know the Good Shepherd through His under-shepherds. But sheep *do* wander off, don't they? I would submit to you that too many sheep are wandering *through* our flocks...

❖ That are hurt but no oil is poured on their wound;
❖ That are never really incorporated into the flock, never feel like they belong and have trouble following along;
❖ Too many that get picked off by wolves

❖ Or fall into ditches
❖ Or off cliffs;
❖ Too many that no shepherd or under-shepherd touched
❖ Too many that no one noticed when they left!

It's the case of the invisible sheep right in front of us. Hollywood's movies usually portray poor morals as the acceptable standard and it makes it hard to enjoy a lot of movies. Once in a while I'll learn of a great illustration in one of them, though. Oddly enough, *What Women Want*[6] had a terrific example of the invisible person. Mel Gibson's character has a run-in with some electricity and it causes him to be able to hear what women are thinking. Yes, I know that's dumb, but go with me for a moment. As he walks through his office he becomes aware of a young clerk no one sees when he "overhears" what she's thinking. She's thinking things like no one even knows she's there ... or cares. It's not that they couldn't if they just looked up, but they don't. He realizes he has never seen her before either, but she's not new! When he asks around to find out her name, no one knows. When he goes out of his way to acknowledge her and be kind, he quite literally saves her life.

Isaiah 40:11 gives us our example:
He tends his flock like a shepherd: He gathers the lambs in his arms and carries them close to his heart; he gently leads those that have young.

That's what Jesus did, and it's exactly what we need to do. The biblical blessing is a terrific tool for doing just that.

*"I
will bless
you;
I will
make your
name great
and you
will be a
blessing."*

Genesis 12:2

Chapter Three
HISTORICAL BACKGROUND

KEY TERMS

Affirmation
Positive confirmation of the inherent value of a person.

Covenant
A contractual agreement between two parties; a compact.

Birthright
The legal and spiritual rights of leadership and inheritance
that are conferred on the firstborn son of the family.

KEY QUESTIONS

- ❖ What is the historical, biblical background?
- ❖ What is a covenant?
- ❖ How is covenant related to blessing?
- ❖ What biblical models or examples are there?
- ❖ What is the biblical imperative relating to blessing?
- ❖ Why is Judah's blessing significant?
- ❖ What does Joseph's blessing illustrate?

From the Beginning

When God created man at the very beginning, His first act toward them was a blessing.

> God blessed them and said to them,
> "Be fruitful and increase in number;
> fill the earth and subdue it.
> Rule over the fish of the sea and the
> birds of the air and over every living
> creature that moves on the ground."
> Genesis 1:28

God loves blessing His people and it is a privilege to participate with Him in it.

The blessings that are our primary pattern in Scripture are given by a parent in the context of acceptance, love and concern. Blessings aren't something that can be earned. On the contrary, they are conferred as a right of birth. They were given by fathers to their sons with no perquisite except membership in the family.

There was a definite spiritual aspect to the blessing as well as physical and material implications. Also, there was a relational aspect to the blessing. The giving of the blessing demonstrated parental love and acceptance.

Our pattern for the biblical blessing comes from the blessings of these fathers, but theirs weren't the first recorded in Scripture. The first blessings and curses were given by God Himself to Adam and Eve, their son, Cain, and then Noah. Centuries later when Abraham came on the scene, Genesis 12:2-3 tells us that God pronounced blessing over him as well.

"I will make you into a great nation and I will bless you;
I will make your name great and you will be a blessing.
I will bless those who bless you,
and whoever curses you I will curse;
and all peoples on earth will be blessed through you."

In that blessing God specifically included the nation that would come from Abraham, and ultimately through him all nations. Then, in Genesis 15, the promise of God's favor was formalized when He made a covenant with Abraham. This covenant was a contractual agreement of favor/blessing that God said would extend to Abraham's seed (offspring) as well. What this literally meant was that the favor God said He would give would be to Abraham's physical, blood related descendants. When a son, Ishmael, was born to Abraham that was outside of God's plan and purpose in the covenant, God gave this son a blessing as well, but he was rejected as the son of the covenant. The covenant son was Isaac and his offspring.

From Abraham, through Isaac and His son Jacob, to Jacob's twelve sons, all the way to Christ, there is one

58

extended family line that is traced through Scripture. The line of that entire family is included in the agreement. This family grew into the Jewish nation of Israel.

After Christ, the covenant was expanded beyond the Jews so all can participate in it by being adopted into the family through Christ. Through Christ, it includes all relationships: spouses, children, family members, friends, or any member of the Christian family. Participation in the blessing of the covenant is the birthright of anyone in the family. Any parent, nurturer, or helper who desires to encourage and lift another can follow the pattern of biblical blessing.

Can a biblical blessing can be given to anyone? Since the blessing has been extended beyond the *original* family of God, you can give a blessing to a person who isn't a Jew or a Christian, but you need to understand that it won't have the same impact. It was given in the framework of blood family, and it is through Christ's blood that we have been adopted. Not only are we adopted by God, as believers in Christ today, we *are blood* family. A non-family member has no way to receive a biblical blessing *fully* because without that blood relationship, the Holy Spirit isn't operational in their lives in the same way. It's the Holy Spirit who conducts the work of God in our lives, and it's only after a person has been made spiritually alive in Christ that the Holy Spirit can give the blessing its full impact. However, a blessing still has the value of drawing them, creating spiritual openness to the Spirit. Indeed, it should be extended beyond our own ranks because its power to tear down blocks furthers the Spirit's access for convicting of sin and the need for Christ.

The practice of blessing was maintained in Orthodox

Judaism through the centuries, father to children. Jewish friends have told me that traditionally, during the Sabbath meal each week, the father of the family blesses each child. What an awesome way to build a child's sense of being loved and valued! Rabbis also follow a similar format when they pronounce the priestly blessing from Numbers 6:24-5 over their congregations. Many Christian ministers have followed the practice as well. It was used as the benediction each week in the church of my childhood.

> *"'" The LORD bless you and keep you;
> the LORD make his face shine upon you
> and be gracious to you;
> the LORD turn his face toward you
> and give you peace." '*

God's footnote in regard to this blessing was a promise:

"So they (the priests, later rabbis & ministers) will put my name on the Israelites, and *I will bless* them."

Biblical Models

Let's look at the biblical models to see how the blessing was given. The first illustration of a formal blessing given by a father to a son is in Genesis 27 - 28:5 where the story of Isaac blessing his two sons occurs.

To fully understand what was involved here, it is necessary to go back a couple of chapters. There were benefits to the first born that uniquely belonged to him. First, there was a double portion of inheritance, called the birthright. Genesis 25: 29-34 indicates that the brother who receives the double portion blessing not only got double the material inheritance, but he would also assume patriarchal leadership of the extended family for that generation, both temporal and spiritual, as well as title to the covenant blessing that God had promised Abraham. If a man had two sons, his estate would be divided into three portions, and the older son would receive two. If there were three sons, the estate would be divided into four portions, and the oldest son would receive two. The oldest son also normally received the father's major blessing. Indeed, the Hebrew word for blessing (*berakah*) is virtually an anagram of the word that means both birthright and firstborn (*bekorah*). Legal continuation of the family line may also have been included among the privileges of the firstborn son. (Holman Bible Dictionary.) In this case, the sons were twins, so the first to emerge gained the birthright. The older twin was Esau. Jacob, even though he was only younger by minutes, was relegated to the lesser position.

Perhaps you remember the story of Esau trading his birthright to his brother Jacob for a meal when he was famished. Clearly, he placed little value on the blessings that would come either from his father or from God. What he was actually doing was trading future long-range blessing for immediate pleasure. It was a foolish choice, which the Bible characterizes as "despising his birthright." Of course, Esau isn't the only person who foolishly made that sort of trade.

61

Eve did virtually the same thing in the garden, and variations of it have happened ever since!

When Isaac is 100 years old and his eyes are so weak he can no longer see, he tells his sons he is going to bless them, apparently thinking his death might be near (he actually lived another 80 years!) Perhaps you remember the story. Jacob is the favorite son of his mother Rebekah. Together they conspire to trick Isaac into giving the blessing of the oldest son to Jacob and they succeed. In Genesis 27:21, Isaac says,

Come near so I can touch you, my son, to know whether you are really my son Esau or not."

The 1st step in the pattern, **positive, concrete contact,** in this case **touch,** is recorded here as well as the beginning of the 2nd, **personal affirmation,** in the use of his name, Esau.

Then, in verse 27, he continues the blessing.

"Ah, the smell of my son is like the smell of a field that the LORD has blessed

the rest of the affirmation.

May God give you of heaven's dew and of earth's richness – an abundance of grain and new wine. May nations serve you and peoples bow down to you. Be lord over your brothers, and may the sons of your mother bow down to you. May those who curse you be cursed and those who bless you be blessed."

The other steps are combined here: **particular words specifically chosen** for him, **painting a vision** of **a future and a hope,** and **partnering follow-through** commitment of the family to him because of his leadership role.

Isaac also blessed Esau when he realized that he'd been tricked by Jacob.

(No doubt also placing his hand on him) Isaac told Esau

Positive, concrete contact – **touch,** and **personal affirmation**

"Your dwelling will be away from the earth's richness, away from the dew of heaven above.

Painting a vision of the future and **giving hope.**

You will live by the sword and you will serve your brother. But when you grow restless, you will throw his yoke from your neck

Partnering for follow-through/ commitment of the family is implied.

The blessing of the land of Canaan was part of the Abrahamic covenant and it went to Jacob. More about the pattern of blessing can be learned from the account of Jacob blesses his sons in Genesis chapters 48 and 49.

A blessing was given to each of his twelve sons and two of the grandsons. In ancient times when extended families remained together, the father held the absolute authority in the family, even after the sons were grown. He was, in short, the head of the clan. His pronouncements were taken as law and binding as such. He had the authority to exercise both temporal and spiritual leadership, acting as both chieftain and priest. If the firstborn was not fit for spiritual or civil leadership of the next generation, the right of the firstborn could be given to another. That's exactly what happened here. Joseph was elevated above his brothers when Ruben was disqualified because of sexual sin with one of his stepmothers, Bilhah.

Genesis 35:22 records that years earlier, not long after Rachel died in childbirth, Jacob moved his family from near Bethlehem farther south to the region of Migdol Eder on the edge of the Negev. Ruben took advantage of what apparently was a tempting situation. Isaac was an old man and his wife Bilhah was no doubt many years younger. He went in and slept with Bilhah, and Jacob heard about it.

Ruben may have believed that he got away with this terrible sin since apparently nothing was said or done about it at the time. Sin always has a way of coming back to haunt us, though, doesn't it? 1 Chronicles 5:1-2 spells it out clearly.

"Reuben, the firstborn of Israel ... but when he defiled his father's marriage bed, his rights as firstborn were given

to the sons of Joseph, son of Israel. So he could not be listed in the genealogical record in accordance with his birthright, and though Judah was the strongest of his brothers and a ruler came from him, the rights of the firstborn belonged to Joseph."

What a contrast to how Joseph behaved when a tempting opportunity presented itself in Potifer's house. Character is what you do when no one is looking. Joseph was not only the most dearly loved son of his father, he was a truly godly man. God blessed him long before his earthly father bestowed his blessing on him. He was given the highest position in the Egypt after the pharaoh himself, and now is given the highest position in the clan by the adoption of his two sons. Genesis 48:5-6 records Jacob saying to Joseph that the two sons who were born to him in Egypt were not going to be reckoned as Joseph's sons any longer, but reckoned as Jacob's. As he put it, "*Ephraim and Manasseh will be mine, just as Reuben and Simeon are mine.*"

When Jacob (Israel) blessed Joseph, the man of God, he did so by blessing Joseph's sons, Ephraim and Manasseh, as part of his own. Through this means he gave Joseph a double blessing, conferring the birthright on him. Jacob put his hands on the sons, but spoke to Joseph. Genesis 48:15-16. Notice the elements of the blessing are all present.

He placed his hands on their heads.	**Positive, concrete contact – touch** (verse14)
Then he blessed Joseph and said,	**Personal affirmation**

"May the God before whom my fathers Abraham and Isaac walked, the God who has been my shepherd all my life to this day, the Angel who has delivered me from all harm --may he bless these boys. May they be called by my name and the names of my fathers Abraham and Isaac, and may they increase greatly upon the earth."

Particular, specific, language chosen especially for them

Then, in Genesis 48:20-22, he continued,

He blessed them that day and said, "In your name will Israel pronounce this blessing: 'May God make you like Ephraim and Manasseh.'" *So he put Ephraim ahead of Manasseh.*

Then Israel said to Joseph, "I am about to die, but God will be with you and take you back to the land of your fathers. And to you, as one who is over your brothers, I give the ridge of land I took from the Amorites with my sword and my bow."

Hope, they were going to be so blessed that being compared to them was going to forever after indicate great blessing!)

Painting a vision for the future.

Partnering support of the family

66

When Jacob uttered these words, as well as the words of blessing spoken in the next chapter, there was a prophetic aspect to it. Ephraim became the largest tribe, inheriting the center of the land, eventually becoming the northern kingdom.

Again he blessed Joseph in chapter 49 when he blessed all his sons. Genesis 49:22-26:

"Joseph is a fruitful vine,
a fruitful vine near a spring, whose
branches climb over a wall.

With bitterness archers
attacked him; They shot at him with
hostility. But his bow remained
steady, His strong arms stayed
limber, because of the hand of the
Mighty One of Jacob, because of
the Shepherd, the Rock of Israel,
because of your father's God, who
helps you, because of the Almighty,
who blesses you with blessings of the
heavens above, blessings of the deep
that lies below, blessings of the
breast and womb.

Your father's blessings are
greater than the blessings of the
ancient mountains, than the bounty
of the age-old hills. Let all these
rest on the head of Joseph, on the
brow of the prince among his
brothers.

Positive, contact – touch implied

Personal affirmation

Particular, specific language

Painting a vision of hope and a future

Partnering support of the family

In chapter 49 Jacob blesses all of his sons one by one in order. The blessing of Joseph above was eleventh. The prophetic element in these blessings is definite and accurate. Since the Holy Spirit is involved when we bless someone, we can find ourselves uttering words that have something of prophecy in them, but it is rather unusual today. In Jacob's case, though, he is pronouncing blessing on the founding fathers of a nation. These men are the heads of what will become the twelve tribes of Israel. It is appropriate that the future of these tribes be given as a means of establishing God's sovereignty.

The blessing of Judah is particularly interesting for us from a prophetic viewpoint. Genesis 49:8-12:

"Judah, your brothers will praise you; your hand will be on the neck of your enemies; your father's sons will bow down to you.
You are a lion's cub, O Judah; you return from the prey, my son.
Like a lion he crouches and lies down, like a lioness— who dares to rouse him?
The scepter will not depart from Judah, nor the ruler's staff from between his feet,

Positive, concrete contact-touch is implied

Personal affirmation – name

Particular, specific words

Painting a hope and a future

Jesus was called the Lion of Judah. He traced His lineage to Judah through Mary by blood and Joseph by adoption. He will be powerful, but is not shown as a raging, ravaging beast. Rather he's shown at peace, enjoying his success and bounty. The kingship was yet in the distant future, but it was given to this tribe here, centuries earlier.

68

until he comes to whom it belongs and the obedience of the nations is his.
He will tether his donkey to a vine, his colt to the choicest branch; he will wash his garments in wine, his robes in the blood of grapes.
His eyes will be darker than wine, his teeth whiter than milk.

A double reference to David and Christ.

Jesus was called both the vine and the fruit of the vine, a drink which symbolizes His blood.

Wait a minute! Isn't Judah the one who was the ringleader among the brothers when they sold Joseph into slavery? Why is God elevating him like this? God recognized his repentance and change of character. When Joseph demanded Benjamin remain in Egypt, Judah begged to take the place of his youngest brother. It would have meant possible slavery for him, but he could not bear the thought that his father lose Rachel's other son, the light of his life. He was willing to lay down his life for his brother. This genuine change of heart caused God to chose Judah's tribe as the line for his own son who would lay down his life for us. As Jesus would be the king, Judah's line was given the future scepter. I imagine this blessing came as quite a surprise to Judah!

What an encouragement for us it is to know that God not only forgives us when we truly repent, but that he will use us and bless us! If God can use a man like Paul, who persecuted and killed Christians for their faith, He can surely use us! Paul is a particularly good example for us because he

69

not only worked as an evangelist, planting new churches, he encouraged, nurtured, and blessed the folks he established in them.

Take a look at the book of 1 Timothy. Usually we emphasize the advice and teaching he sent young pastor Timothy, but the letter is also full of blessing. Obviously he couldn't physically touch him from a distance, but in 1:2 he says the letter is to "Timothy, my *true son*." This greeting is a statement in which he places value on Timothy in a way that seems to me rather like a written hug!

He uses language specifically chosen to help and encourage Timothy. These words are both practical and appropriate to his challenges and situation. Next, he affirms Timothy's hope and future when he tells him in 4:6 that if he teaches the things his people need to know, he will be "a good minister of Christ Jesus. Then in 5:17 he says that the elders who direct the work of the church, especially those who preach and teach (i.e. Timothy), are *well worthy* of double honor! Does that remind you of anything? Think of Joseph and the double blessing. Paul is saying here that Timothy is going to have an impact on his church worthy of a double blessing! He refers to him as a man of God in 6:11, clearly worthy of the commitment Paul expresses in 3:14-15 where he reminds Timothy that he is coming to see him to further help with the teaching and nurturing of the church. This whole letter overflows with blessing for Timothy, the man of God.

While prophecies like that of Jacob about his family are way outside the norm of most of the blessings we give, remember that the Holy Spirit is the one choosing the specific language as we request it of Him. Don't be surprised if He says something through you that you don't entirely expect!

"...God
...who comforts us

...so that
we can
comfort

those
in any
trouble."

2 Corinthians 1:4

Chapter Four
THE NEED FOR BLESSING

KEY TERMS

Acceptance
Favorable reception; approval; favor.

Pessimist
A person who habitually sees or anticipates the worst or is disposed to be gloomy.

Support system
A network of family, friends or an organization(s) that work to help, encourage, and aid.

KEY QUESTIONS

- ❖ Who needs a blessing?
- ❖ Why is it needed?
- ❖ What is the biblical imperative?
- ❖ What is God's field or His building?
- ❖ What is the field's significance for us?
- ❖ How do Romans 12:4–5 and Ephesians 2:22 relate to the need for blessing?

Why do you need to know how to incorporate blessing language into your conversation and ministry? It touches people at their point of need.

Who Needs a Blessing?

Well, for a starter, how about people who could use a hug? Perhaps you're not a "hugger" by nature, so this idea might seem a bit foreign to you. For those of you who are, you are probably well aware of how people respond to a hug. There is a brightening of the face, a warming of the attitude, a relaxing of barriers.

I remember the first time my expressive, Italian friend, Carmela, greeted me with a hug. I didn't know it yet, but she is a Hugger with a capitol H. I came into Bible study that morning feeling well...o.k. Not great you understand, just o.k. You've had mornings like that, haven't you? A lot of little things went wrong, but nothing big enough that I could really justify complaining about it. It was just the usual – kids not ready for school quite on time, car keys misplaced, a phone call when I could finally dash out the door that I didn't have enough sense to ignore! I arrived feeling slightly out of sorts just as things were getting started. Not really noticing the greeters at the door, I walked into the room right past Carmela, when her hand reached and gently grabbed my arm.

"Teresa! How are you?"
She wrapped me in a warm embrace, and whispered in my ear, "I love you, girl."

As the frustration of my morning faded, I remember saying, "Thanks, I needed that." And I did! I just hadn't realized it. Now I make a point of walking her way! Even on days when I'm better than o. k., a hug gives me a lift. I've wondered if it will ever seem too much, but I have never found my hug limit!

Several years ago I was part of a symposium for women in ministry. Another woman and I who part of the staff were asked to greet at the entrance to the chapel where the main sessions were held. As the women approached the doors, I began to welcome the ladies with a greeting and a hug. My friend co-worker saw what I was doing and followed suit. At first the ladies were a bit surprised and rather stiff, though they reacted rather like I had with Carmela, warming to the embrace. The next session, the ladies made a beeline for us to get their hugs, refusing to pass without one. By the third session there was a line because everyone wanted to be hugged by both of us! Over and over these mature women in ministry said they were amazed at how wonderful it felt to be hugged like that. Several said they had never experienced anything like it and thanked us again and again. We made a lot of hugging converts that day!

God has comforted us when we needed it, and we do well to pass along the favor.

"...God ...who comforts us ...so that we can comfort those in any trouble." 2 Corinthians 1:4

Who else needs a blessing? People who didn't receive enough acceptance from their parents are in great need. These folks most certainly didn't receive their parents' blessing. The love many received from their parents was conditional, with excessive expectations, unrealistic or constantly rising demands. When the parent(s) in this kind of home decides that   the child does *exactly* what is considered good, he is acceptable. The problem is that often there is inconsistency about what good means,, and even when the child is good, it may not be good enough. There is often insensitivity, indifference or absence on the part of the parent.

I was speaking at a woman's retreat one week-end, when a young woman approached me after a session. She told me she was raped by a family member, but when she told her parents, they didn't believe her. They said they "knew" he wouldn't do something like that, and she *misunderstood* what had happened. If she had a problem with him, if *anything* did happen, it was no doubt her fault. Not surprisingly, the young woman who stood before me had self-esteem that was nearly non-existent. She's not the only woman who's told me a variation on that story.

Every once in a while I run across a story in the newspaper of a student who has committed suicide because his grades weren't high enough to meet his parents expectations. I remember one in particular in which the youngster has getting his lowest mark ever and couldn't bear it. ...It was a B.

Sadly, wounds that stem from that lack of acceptance heal poorly, if they heal at all. It's amazing how many people you meet who have this sort of experience growing up in common. Just this week a friend mentioned to me that she was dating a terrific Christian guy. Her comment about him was that they got along incredibly well because they both came from super critical homes! They understand the tendency to duck and run for cover and problems of self-worth. They each still struggle with the results of constant criticism though they are adults of middle years.

Don't be deceived into thinking that just because someone comes from a Christian home that there couldn't have been a lot of criticism and a distinct lack of acceptance there, that standards couldn't have been unreasonable or unattainable.

A woman I know who grew up in a "Christian" home like that called one day all excited with "Big news!"

"Teresa, guess what? You'll never believe it! Are you sitting down?"

Why do people say that? Did she think I'd fall over from the impact? I couldn't begin to imagine what could have her so excited. A new car? A better job?

"My dad called this morning and told me he was proud of how I'm doing! Can you believe it? I'm just waiting for the other shoe to drop."

It did. Later, she called back and said she had talked to him again. He went right back to his list of everything he thought was under par about her.

"Oh, well. It was nice while it lasted..."

Do you know someone like that? Perhaps you're thinking of your own family experience.

As believers, the Word says that we are accepted by God,

"...Having predestined us unto the adoption of children by Jesus Christ to himself, ...wherein he hath made us accepted in the beloved." Ephesians 1:5-6 (KJV)

We can pass on that assurance to those believers who don't have it. It's often been said that we are God's hands and feet. As we fully accept and establish what is lacking in a life, the ability to receive God's acceptance grows.

Then there are the people who are discouraged or need encouragement. Scripture exhorts us to:

"Encourage one another daily..." Hebrews 3:13

How often? Daily seems rather overboard, some would say. I don't think so. I suspect this admonition is given because everyone really needs encouragement on a frequent, regular basis. I know it lifts my spirit when someone tells me I'm doing a good job. How about you?

There are also people who need their hope renewed.

"Where there is no vision, the people perish."
Proverbs 29:18 (KJV)

I have a missionary friend, Lila Townsend, who illustrated for me just how true this is. When she and her family were establishing a church in Moscow, she said that she was immediately struck by the cheerless, oppressive atmosphere. Over time she observed that the Russian people have an extraordinarily bleak an outlook on life. Their daily life includes a frequently futile search for enough food and any other necessity they need. The godless system under which they have grown up has made them great pessimists ... a people with little or no vision or hope. She said there is even a universal scowl that all the people wear on the street. Hopelessness is the standard attitude.

Then there are the multitudes of people who feel lonely or unloved, who desperately need attention and love.

79

It has always amazed me that it is possible to feel alone in a crowd. I've felt that way. Have you? It is a common, though unwelcome feeling for so many, many people today. The majority of us don't live where we grew up. Many have little or no family near by. The fact that we can be a mobile society has many economic advantages, but it means that many have moved away from the comforting support of family and friends.. We lose the network of support, or our support system, when we move, and unfortunately, many are never able to really replace it. Ours is a society of fences and walls in most places. The neighborliness of small town America just doesn't exist for most of us. The result is we feel separated from those we love and who love us. But that's not the way Jesus intends for us to live. He says,

"As I have loved you, so love one another."
John 13:34

Sharon Moshivi[7] is a writer living in Tokyo. She read a commentary she wrote on the radio that pointed out this very thing. She discovered that the Japanese have a cultural taboo against making eye contact with a stranger. She found no one would acknowledge her presence, her existence even. People would step around her in public like she was a post. When an approaching person moved in order to pass and she inadvertently moved the same way, and that funny little side stepping dance occurred, there was no quick smile. When she tried to make eye contact, they looked right through her...like she was invisible. Clerks would even do business with her like she wasn't there!

She quoted the introduction of Ralph Ellison's book, The Invisible Man,[8] as stating exactly what she experienced. "I am invisible, understand, because people refuse to see me."

Soon, Sharon began to find that acknowledgment of her presence, even by strangers, was important to her self-esteem. "It felt like pieces of myself were fading away," she said. Though she was strong enough to reject the thought, she couldn't help thinking, "Perhaps it is true; perhaps I am invisible." It sounds like the fictional character in the movie, *What Women Want*, doesn't it? Think how lonely it would make you feel.

So, who needs to be blessed? Those who need a hug, who need acceptance or encouragement, who need hope, or who are lonely. Everybody needs to be blessed! And, **why do they need it?** For all the obvious reasons, but in addition, as believers we are all parts of one body.

Just as each of us has one body with many members, and these members do not all have the same function, so in Christ we who are many form one body, and each member belongs to all the others. Romans 12: 4-5

God intended that we all work together toward the common goal of establishing and growing His kingdom. When one part of the body is hurting, the whole is effected.

" *We are being* built ***together*** *to become a dwelling in which God lives by His Spirit.* " Ephesians 2: 22

We need to view our interactions as a joint building project. If a wall or some other part is weak or crumbling, if

81

the development is delayed or blocked, the whole project is effected by it.

Think of the building projects you've known of in the natural realm. One glitch can cause the whole project to be held up. One thing out of alignment causes a whole area to be out of sync and the difficulty acts like a ripple in a pond. The influence can be felt out to the edges.

When John Donne said, "No man is an island, entire of itself," he was right. "Every man is a piece of the continent, a part of the main."[9] We are one building, one body, connected by the common blood of Christ, with the same Spirit flowing through us.

The Biblical Imperative

"Therefore encourage one another and build each other up." 1 Thessalonians 5: 11

As we noted before, this is to be done on a daily basis, not once in a blue moon, and not simply if it happens to cross your mind or if it's convenient, or if you feel like it!

"For we are God's fellow workers; you are God's field, God's building. By the grace God has given me, I laid a foundation as an expert builder, and someone else is building on it. But each one should be careful how he builds. ...If what he built survives, he will receive his reward. If it is burned up, he will suffer loss; he himself will be saved, but only as one escaping through the flames. Don't you know that you yourselves are God's temple and that God's Spirit lives in you?"
1 Corinthians 3: 10,14-16"

We're not working on just any old building project. We are corporately God's temple, as well as individual temples where He dwells. We are like mobile chapels, small temples that can walk. When we gather together, we become like parts of a greater whole, yet God's dwelling isn't diminished when we are apart. Amazing, isn't it? Aren't you glad that what we're called to do is be obedient to the directions of the Holy Spirit, our foreman, rather than being responsible for building when we can't see the entire plan? He provides the tools and materials, the skill and the wisdom to get the job done. Giving the blessing is a skill he can teach us to use with great effectiveness in His building program.

Pastor G. L. Johnson, Peoples Church, Fresno, my pastor, has been preaching through Exodus. As he talked about the making of the tabernacle, he mentioned all the variety of things the people contributed and did for the project, making the point that we all have a role to play in the building of God's kingdom (building) in our time. As he described the cloud of God's presence filling the tent, I got to thinking. God dwells in our *temple*, but John 1:14 expresses it a little differently. It says that The Word became flesh and made His dwelling among us. I remembered a word study I did one time in which I learned that "made His dwelling among us" in the Greek was literally "tabernacled." Jesus tabernacled among us. He pitched His tent here for awhile.

When my grandfather went home to be with the Lord, my mom and grandmother wanted an open casket. Others in the family overruled on the grounds that some might find a corpse frightening. I'll never forget the wistfulness in mom's voice when she and grandma consoled each other later. Mom said, "I know it was just his old tent, but it was precious to us and we wanted to see it as long as possible." They knew as believers we are the temple (tabernacle) of the Holy Spirit. They had no fear or revulsion of that dear, old tent when grandpa's spirit and the Holy Spirit left it behind. It wasn't needed anymore.

Jesus' tent was filled with the presence of God just like the tabernacle in the wilderness. Now our tents are filled with God's presence as well. The glory of His presence needs to shine through all we do. Until we leave our tents empty behind us, we have a biblical imperative to work on the building of the kingdom, to pass on the blessing that invites, encourages, and contributes to new construction.

Part Two
Aspects of
Biblical Blessing

*"...He tends
His flock
like a shepherd;
He gathers
the lambs
in His arms
and carries them
close to His
heart..."*

Isaiah 40:11

Chapter Five
PURPOSEFUL, DEFINITE CONTACT

KEY TERMS

Touch
Physical contact, especially of hands or fingers, laying on of hands.

Commissioned
Officially charged and delegated to specific service with authorization to perform the duties thereof.

Empowered
Given authorization; enabled to perform; given strength.

Sodality
A frame of reference based on experience; a particular way of perceiving something, like an architect's blueprint as a way of viewing a house.

KEY QUESTIONS

- ❖ How is Jehovah unique?
- ❖ What's different about Christianity?
- ❖ How does this compare to non-Christian religions?
- ❖ How does God reach out to man?
- ❖ Why is touch important?
- ❖ How does touch affect people?

The Tangible Love of God

When my son Tyler was small, he became frightened at bedtime one night. I assured him that Jesus was there and He would protect him.

"Where is He? Ty asked, still afraid. "I can't see Him or feel Him." I explained in 4 year old language that when we ask Jesus into our hearts, He lives inside of us. I prayed with him about Jesus coming in, and then Ty said, "Good. Now if any bad people come in here, I'll open my mouth real wide and Jesus can reach out and sock 'em!"

People want a tangible expression of God's presence, of His love and care for them. Like the proverbial story of the child who was frightened in the night and when reassured about Jesus like Ty was, told her parents she needed some love with skin on!

I'm told the great theologian, Karl Barth, was once asked what the most profound truth he ever heard was. His reply was simply this: "Jesus loves me." I'm sure his listeners were expecting a lofty and complicated answer, but instead he gave the same one that every Sunday school child could give. It is the *foundational truth* of the faith. The first song I can remember learning in Sunday school and the first one I taught my children was "Jesus Loves Me."[10] It's that last song I sang to Lisa on the afternoon she lay dying, the only one I thought some remote part of her might still remember.

Likewise, the first verse most of us learned was John 3:16, "For God so *loved* the world that He *gave* His one and only Son…" Nothing is more important than the love of God, and there is nothing that people need more. However, I suspect most of us feel like Ty and that little child in the story ~ we need something more tangible, love with some skin on!

Of course, the reality in our time is that Jesus is no longer here on earth where He can touch people in the flesh. Now the only love of God with skin on is the love He extends through us.

It is through our hands He touches and blesses.
If we really understood how *great* God's desire
to reach out and touch people was,
it seems to me
there'd be a whole lot of huggin' going on!

If we are going to extend God's touch and blessing, it's helpful to think through just why and how God touches us.

The God Who Comes to Man

Have you ever pondered how truly unique Christianity is compared to the other religions of mankind? There are a lot of specifics that we could compare, but by far the most significant is that w e serve the only God who comes to man.

From the very beginning, God sought out the children of his heart. Do you remember how the Garden of Eden is described in Genesis chapter 3? When I try to visualize it, I imagine a lush greenness accented by brilliant flowers and birds. There must have been the music of waterfalls and birdsong, as well as the gentle calls of animals filling the air. Adam and Eve had no cares or worries there, no want of food, no fears for life or the future. Until. . . . the serpent tempted them and they fell.

When their eyes were opened to their nakedness, their sin, shame came to them. The Word says that God's custom was to walk in the garden in the cool of the day where He would meet with them. (Genesis 2:8) But on this day they were afraid, though they never had been before, and they hid themselves from God. The wonderful trees of the garden no longer were seen as a source of beauty and food, but instead became things to hide behind. But God missed them, missed their company and fellowship. He called to them, "Where are you?" When they didn't come to Him, He sought them. When they withdrew from Him, He reached out to them. When they hid, He called. He has been seeking, reaching, calling ever since.

Jehovah is unlike any other god that humans worship.
He is the God who comes to man.

How is Jehovah unique?

When God told Moses to Go to Egypt and lead His people to freedom, Moses worried that the Hebrews wouldn't listen to him, let alone follow him. After all, it had been forty years since he had been in Egypt, and he hadn't left under the best circumstances.. Besides, when Moses tried to stand up for them against an abusive Egyptian, look how that had ended! Not only were they not grateful that he took their side, they rejected him. The Pharaoh who had tried to kill

Moses over that incident had since died, but it certainly must have occurred to Moses that someone might remember and cause problems, even after all this time. Surely there was someone better for the job! As Moses put it in Exodus 3:11, "Who am I that I should to go to Pharaoh to bring the Israelites out of Egypt?"

Who, indeed? What Moses didn't realize yet was that the point wasn't who he was, but who God is. God replied to his question with two revelations that are as significant for us today as they were for Moses then.

First, God promised to be with him. He was sending Moses into a dangerous situation for a completely daunting purpose, but He wasn't asking him to go alone. Not since the time of Enoch who walked with God, had such a relationship been even hinted at. This God who spoke to Moses was different than any he had ever known about. What kind of God can actually be with you? Remember, Moses was talking to a burning bush at the time. Was the bush going to move? That might seem silly to you, but how much odder is that than a bush that burns but isn't consumed, or a bush with a voice coming out of it?

He still didn't quite understand this new relationship because he immediately asked who he should tell the Israelites had *sent* him. God reveled His name to Moses, which explained something of His nature, His ability to go with him. He said, "I AM WHO I AM. " He was then instructed to tell Israelites that I AM has sent him to them, and to tell them that He was the same God their fathers had known. In fact, He was thereafter often called The LORD (Jehovah-English, Yahweh or YHWH - Hebrew), the God of our fathers - the God of Abraham, the God of Isaac and the God of Jacob.

94

God concluded with this declaration: "This is my name forever, the name by which I am to be remembered from generation to generation . . . I have surely visited you . . ." Exodus 3:14-15,16

What does I AM WHO I AM mean, anyway? Matthew Henry's Commentary[11] explains the expression means He is self-existent: He has His being in and of Himself. It means that He is eternal and unchangeable, and always the same, yesterday, today, and forever. He is incomprehensible; we cannot by searching find Him out. This name, as Henry so aptly puts it, "checks all bold and curious inquiries concerning God. He is faithful and true to all His promises, unchangeable in His Word as well as in His nature."

Contrast this explanation of God with what you know about idols, the other gods. Idols are products of man's imagination as well as the inspiration and deception of Satan. They are not alive, despite claims or surface appearances to the contrary. They are deaf, dumb, blind, cold, in short, dead. Their ordinances are instituted by men with the help and encouragement of Satan.

The very existence of other gods is due to rebellion. Satan was the first rebel, and 1/3 of Heaven's angels followed him in his rebellion. Adam and Eve unwittingly followed his example as well when they yielded to temptation. Their sin resulted in the fall and a fundamental change in the nature human beings and what would be passed down to us as their offspring. God's nature was supplanted by the sin nature.

Our heritage is a life-long battle with sin that arises out of our own nature, as well as a predisposition to fall for temptation. There is an on-going battle with temptation that on our own we can't win.

But, God's attitude toward us has always remained faithful even when mankind wasn't. He didn't give up on us. He kept on reaching.

Several years ago Bill and Gloria Gaither wrote a Christmas song about this very thing.

"His Love Reaching"[12]

The narration begins, "Right from the beginning God's love has *reached,* and from the beginning man has refused to understand. But Love went on reaching, risking rejection, offering itself...."

The lyrics spell it out so beautifully:

Love went on...Searching,
      ...Longing,
         ...Reaching

"And Love went on reaching
Right past the shackles of my mind...

And His Love
      reached all the way to where I was."

Of all those who are called gods, only Jehovah God, the I AM, reaches out to man in love. But why?

Why does he reach out? Ah, the answer lies in His nature. He has a desire for relationship with us because the very essence of His nature is relationship. He is God the Father, God the Son, and God the Holy Spirit. How very natural then that He has an interest from multiple, relational points of view.

First and foremost, He has a **paternal** interest in us.. He has a father's love for His children, a father's longing to know us, a father's concern for our welfare and well-being.

He also has a **fraternal** interest. As God the Son He desires to be our elder brother.

His **internal** interest comes from the fact that He is God the Holy Spirit. He desires to indwell us, to have intimate, constant fellowship.

He desires that we be a part of His **extended family**. He enables us to come alongside Him and become adopted children in the family of God, in relationship to Him as part of the corporate whole.

God's desire for relationship with us does indeed arise out of His nature because the sum total of His nature is love. It is this love that provides the motivation for His reaching ~ the motivation of love

Many people misunderstand what love actually is:. At its root it is a *conscious decision* to be *for* someone, to have his best interest and welfare at heart. Love is often mistaken for affection but it is much more.

❖ Love is not an emotion (though it can and does produce emotion.)
❖ Love cannot be separated from commitment.
❖ Love leads to action. The proof of love is in the follow-through.

One of the interesting dilemmas of many modern relationships is the inability of one or both partners to actually say the words "I love you." Lovers can have lots of emotional spark, have sexual intimacy, perhaps even be living together, but not be committed to one another. Inevitably the relationship will fail where committed partnering for support is missing. Love and emotion are connected but not the same thing. Emotions are essentially reactions to people or

97

situations. Love will produce emotions, but emotions don't necessarily produce love. Love, contrary to the popular use of the word, is a bond of unqualified acceptance and commitment.

When parents hold their newborn child for the first time and really look at him, what they experience is genuine love. Their love isn't a response to his beauty (most newborns don't look like the Gerber baby just yet!) or anything he has done (which at this point is exactly nothing.) What they see is something that came from them, an extension of themselves. It is something which they birthed. Love is the same. It is something you birth, an extension of who you are. Just as in natural birth, it is the outcome of a decision and an action that is rooted in who you are. How fascinating that love arises out of who you are, yet is fundamentally selfless. It is completely others oriented.

Man's capacity for genuine love undoubtedly diminished when sin entered the world, because sin brought selfishness. *But,* our capacity to love was redeemed and restored in Christ. We now have the potential to love lavishly as God does. We love, as 1 John 4 explains, because of God first loving us. He is love, and as He lives in us, His love lives (is birthed) in us. Then, as we choose to extend that love, it is birthed into the lives of others. It is a natural outcome supernaturally accomplished.

Like all birth, it is a miracle.

Because of the motivation of His genuine love and commitment, God does have emotional involvement with us. This is an important point to make, because God's love for us is not some abstract, unemotional, detached thing. Most non-Christian religions do not envision a God of love, but even when they do, it is not a God of love who *is involved* with them. The God of the Bible is not a distant, abstract force for good. He is the God who reached out to connect with man, and kept on reaching until He could complete the connection with us through Jesus.

This is clearly evident in at least four ways::

❖ **Feelings:** God has feelings of compassion for our distress, disappointment and heartache, or anger when we are disobedient. Likewise, He feels joy when we obey.

It's easy to find examples of the Father's anger. See Hebrews 3:17, Exodus 14:24, or Deuteronomy 29:27-28.

Jesus ' emotions toward us are even easier to spot. Think of His disappointment and heartache when He cried over Jerusalem's rejection (Matthew 23:37), or His grief at the death of His friend Lazarus. John 11:43 I can imagine the fury in His voice at the misuse of His father's house as John recorded the cleansing of the temple in chapter 2 verse 15. He said "How *dare* you make my Father's house into a market!"

The emotions cover the full spectrum. Jesus and His Father were often moved with compassion. Jeremiah 42:12, Matthew 14:14. Proverbs 11:20 and Isaiah 68:16 records the Father's joy and delight over His people, Luke 1:14 the Shepherd's joy at finding His lost sheep.

❖ **Caring** : God's emotions are demonstrated in His Caring for us.

John 11:38 said of Jesus coming to Lazarus' tomb that He "was deeply moved." He cared that Lazarus had suffered. He cared that He had died. He cared that Mary and Martha were grieving. He grieved, too. He couldn't help

99

it. He cared ... so much that He wept. ... so much that He gave His life for ours. He took our sin and grief upon Himself and paid the price for them. Isaiah 53-4-5

❖ **Giving:** God's emotional involvement with us is also obvious in the giving of God to us.

God has been giving to us throughout all of recorded history, giving us His ultimate gift, Jesus Himself. But He didn't do it alone. Jesus participated in the decision. He voluntarily laid down His life.

We really could have asked for no more. The gift of eternal life is no small thing. If would have been gift enough, no, more than enough. But a parent who loves does more than give life. He gives everything that is necessary for life to grow and flourish.

Annie Johnson's old hymn [13] puts it so well:

> "His love has no limit;
> His grace has measure;
> His pow'r has no boundary
> known unto men.
> For out of His infinite riches in Jesus,
> He giveth, and giveth, and giveth again!"

❖ **Chastising:** God chastises us for disobedience so that when we respond the wonderful result for us is reconciliation with Him.

OK, so how is Christianity different than other religions? In non-Christian religions having some conception of a deity, man does the reaching out to the god. Man has the full responsibility of trying to measure up, to reach the god that is being worshipped. The catch is the standards are impossible to meet, no matter how hard you try, and there is no divine help for man in meeting them.

There is also a demand for conformity in most of these religious systems. For the most part, the motivation for obedience is not love but fear of the consequences of disobedience. This is true fear, not reverential awe. Often the fear includes a very real (and realistic) fear of the human religious authorities that speak for and govern on behalf of the god. There can be a kind of one-size-fits-all approach. The individual isn't valued as one who was made in the image of God and loved as such. Women are particularly vulnerable in many of these religious systems. Even today, there are religions in which adherents obey because their lives are in jeopardy if they don't. The world had a dramatic lesson in this very thing as the spotlight of attention fell on the Talliban in Afghanistan.

Of course, there are usually rewards associated with non-Christian religions, but they tend to be illusive, illusionary, unequally distributed and / or temporary. The cost of acceptance tends to go up and up, with no assurance that the requirement has ever been satisfied.

The demand for conformity has an external element. The god's of other religions do not have personal relationships with people. They are distant, not beings that have fellowship with their people. Even in the case of a person who has a demonic spirit, there is no real relationship, no

101

internal unity. A person with a demon can even be unaware of it!

Second, there is also a legalistic aspect to this demand for conformity. Since there is no relationship with the god, there can be no personal interaction and no individual application. Instead, there are commands and possible future rewards, but individual variance is not allowed. The god does not work with one person one way, and with another some other way. There is a kind of one-size-fits-all approach.

In contrast, our call to obedience is a call to follow principles that are for our good. They work to make us successful, safe, healthy, and happy. They aren't legalistic rules instituted for arbitrary uniformity or the convenience of men. We obey not because we have no choice or out of cowering fear, but out of gratitude for the relationship God has granted us through the salvation Jesus provided.

What about instances where a god seems to be alive? What is happening? Is it possible that any of these other gods are actually alive? Only in a manner of speaking. The god itself isn't alive, but a demonic force can make it appear so. The only life in the gods of this world is the demonic force of Satan behind it.

> Jehovah is alive, bringing people to **life**;
> Satan is also alive, but he is a force for **death**.

The demonic forces under Satan's control ape God's actions to deceive the unwary and vulnerable. In Western culture this deception doesn't usually present itself as something so archaic as a literal idol. Most believe themselves much too sophisticated to believe in something like that, but many are drawn to the more fashionable spiritual entities who are "out there" that they believe are going to give them special information, insight, or help of some kind. Mother earth (goddess) worship, Wicca (white witchcraft), and New Age spiritualism have gained a real foothold in recent years. Palm readers, astrologers, Tarot card readers, and mediums are more popular than ever. There are even ads on television now for phone-in readings. The ultimate, though, is the television show that features a medium talking to the dead! Who is he talking to? Not who they think! There is a real spiritual entity involved, all right, but it's not the dear departed. Demons have been listening and watching their assigned targets and can give out details the medium couldn't know . *Of course* there is a reality to what the medium reveals. It's the same with the spiritual elements of all the non-biblical religious and quasi-religious activities. Genuinely supernatural things *really do* happen, but they are aren't what they seem. Their purpose is to deceive people so as to lure them away from the truth and blessing of God. These deceptions are effective because they are cons tailor-made for the mark. They are designer productions! They particularly target the areas of hurt and desire where people are most vulnerable, focusing on the emotions to aid believability. Any good that comes from these encounters or from the worship of any other god is temporary at best, and ultimately a snare for destruction.

103

Satan most definitely reaches out to man, but he doesn't reach in love.

He has no desire to bring about what is best for us. On the contrary, the Bible says he is a "roaring lion, seeking whom he may devour." 1Peter 5:8 His whole goal is to tear people down, and by any means possible, bring about their earthly and eternal destruction.

The fruit or produce of a life reveals its nature:

Giving, Birthing, Building and Blessing

God
vs.
Satan

Stealing, Killing, Destroying and Cursing

God reaches out to us because of His great love to give us life, to help us grow and become fully mature. He wants to have fellowship with us and to bless us. That's the why of reaching. The next logical question is how?

How Does God Reach Out?

His reaching is inherently active. Wouldn't it have been awesome to have walked with Him in the Garden of Eden in the cool of the day? Walking **side by side** we would have had an entirely different experience of His presence. When we paused and turned toward Him, we would have **seen** (visual) Him face to face, up close and personal. Just as Adam and Eve dealt with Him as intimates, we too would be able to speak directly and **hear** (audible) the reply with our physical ears. It was originally a tangible relationship.

Just think, instead of only hearing a still small voice, they were actually able to *hear* Him speak, and talk with Him the same! God's reaching was a real and tangible experience.

God's reaching in the Old Testament was tangible in other ways as well. Remember when Noah finally entered the ark after working on it for a 100 years? God closed the ark door Himself, Genesis 7:16 tells us. Then there was Abraham who served three men who **ate** a meal in his camp in chapter 18. One of them is referred to as the LORD in our English translations, which is Jehovah or Yahweh in Hebrew. Many scholars believe this was the pre-incarnate Christ. It reminds me of Rev. 3:20 where Jesus says that if we open our door to Him, He will come in and eat with us.

Moses had a tangible experience with God, too. After he spent time in God's presence, he bore the evidence of a glowing **face.** He was in the presence of the shekinah glory to such a degree that his face had to be covered because he frightened the people! Now there's a goal worth pursuing...

to be in the Lord's presence so completely that there is a glow about us!

God also reached out in tangible ways through heavenly messengers. The two men who accompanied Jehovah on the visit to Abraham and ate a meal there were angels. They went on from there to Sodom in chapter 19 and lodged for the night with Lot, Abraham's nephew. In the morning they **grasped his hand** to hurry him and his family out of the city before God destroyed it.

Mary's experience is something we're reminded of each Christmas as we read Luke chapter 1. When Gabriel visited her to announce Jesus' coming, she both **saw** and **heard** him. Before he visited Mary he talked to Zechariah in the temple to tell of John the Baptist's coming.

Another method God uses to reach out to men is through dreams. Both of the Josephs in scripture experienced God's reaching through dreams in Genesis 40-41 and Matthew 2.

God also reaches out through appointed, anointed people. Think of the prophets Elisha, Isaiah, Jeremiah, Daniel, and so many others. Kings like David and Joash come to mind as well.

Most important of all, He reached out through Jesus. God sent His Son bodily into the world.

Perhaps the most precious characterizations of Jesus are as the Good Shepherd. The shepherd analogies illustrate a number of different ways God makes contact with us.

❖ He leads and guides us in the 23rd Psalm:

He leads me beside quiet waters ... He guides me in paths of righteousness for His name's sake.

❖ He carries us:

*...He tends his flock like a shepherd; He **gathers the lambs in his arms and carries them close to his heart**...*" Isaiah 40:11

❖ He lays down His life:

*"...I am the good shepherd. The good shepherd **lays down his life** for the sheep.*" John 10:11 '

When Jesus ministered, positive, concrete, yet gentle physical contact was an important and consistent part. His touch was a tender gesture that people easily understood when He placed His hands on the children.

*'Jesus said, 'Let the little children come to me, and do not hinder them, for the kingdom of heaven belongs to such as these.' When he had placed his **hands** on them, he went on from there.*" Matthew 19:14-15

Jesus didn't restrict His touch to just the darling little ones that *none* of us can resist.. Matthew 8:2 tells the story of a repulsive leper whose flesh was decaying before its time. He boldly declared that Jesus could heal Him if He was willing (such faith!) and Jesus responded by extending His hand and touching the horror in front of Him. "I am willing."

When God gives us opportunity to touch someone on His behalf, remember the leper. He didn't focus on the destruction sin was wreaking, but looked beyond it to the precious one inside. It isn't an easy thing to learn to do, but we can with His help. Have you ever picked up a baby whose clothes are drenched in urine and whose dirty diaper has added disgustingly to the mess? How do we find it possible to do that? We may not volunteer for such a chore, but we know there is a precious baby under all that vile mess. We don't focus on what is, but what will be as soon as we get him washed, changed, and the sweet fragrance of powder replaces the stench! That's how God sees us, and He never recoils from *our* mess. He may never have you touch someone who's outside is as horrifying as a leper, but if He does you can be confident that there is purpose and healing in His touch.

God reached out by all these means, and now He reaches out through believers who are commissioned and authorized to reach out to a waiting world on His behalf.

> "Then Jesus came to them and said,
> 'All authority in heaven and on earth has been given to me. Therefore go and make disciples of all nations, baptizing them in the name of the Father and of the Son and of the Holy Spirit, teaching them to obey everything I have commanded you...."
> Matthew 28:18-20

Jesus' conversation with Peter after His resurrection further urges us. In response to Peter's affirmations that He truly loved Him, Jesus told him to feed His lambs, to take care of my sheep, to feed His sheep. John 21: 15b, 16b, 17b We are commissioned to reach out for Him.

The good news is that He never expected us to attempt the rather daunting task of reaching on our own.

❖ He provides direction:

"I tell you the truth, anyone who has faith in me will do what I have been doing." John 14:12a

❖ He provides a teacher:

...But the counselor, the Holy Spirit, whom the Father will send in my name, will teach you all things and will remind you of everything I have said to you." John 14:26

❖ He provides the empowering:

*"'Again Jesus said, 'Peace be with you! As the Father has sent me, I am sending you.' And with that he breathed on them and said, 'Receive the **Holy Spirit**.'"* John 20: 21-22

What is the role of the Holy Spirit in all of this? A strategic one. He is involved with each opportunity God gives us because the Holy Spirit facilitates God's will in the earth. He brings the awareness of the need before us, the love and compassion for the person we are to reach, the opportunity, the comfort we are to offer, the insight into what

109

we are to say, and so on. He is absolutely vital to our reaching out in blessing.

God's reaching is the foundation and motivation for our reaching in His name. While God's reaching was accomplished in several ways, our reaching involves positive, concrete contacts that will usually be a physical touch.

The child who wanted some love with skin on represents all of us. We all need a warm embrace.

The Warm Embrace

There is an emotional aspect to being touched. It affects our sense of well being, our sense of security. It's a tangible demonstration of being loved. People who live alone or are widowed take on new sparkle and life when someone gives them a hug. Just as my Italian friend Carmela makes me feel special when she goes out of her way to hug me, I am conscious that there are other noticeable changes in me. I truly *feel* better, happier, lighter and more carefree. It's like a tonic, good for whatever ails my emotions.

There have been numerous studies on how import physical contact is for people, and nowhere is it more important than for little ones. It is essential to proper growth and development. Babies who are not picked up and cuddled fail to thrive and can die, even if they receive sufficient nourishment. I was moved beyond words a number of years ago when I watched a documentary about a Russian orphanage that was overloaded with babies and small children, but desperately short of staff. One weary nurse described how children who were never touched except to be changed (rarely) and given a bottle (which the child often had to hold alone) were simply existing, but not developing.

College students from our church have been making missions trips to Bucharest, Romania, and have experienced the orphanage syndrome firsthand. The ministry they travel there to support runs an orphanage, but even with Christians in charge, being short-staffed takes its toll. The children can't get enough hugging and holding. Our kids could hardly bear to leave, and at least three have gone back for longer terms.

Isn't it tragic that because of the abuse of a few in the realm of touch, no one in the public arena can safely give a child a hug or a pat on the shoulder? Kids need to be touched, and many aren't touched in blessing by their parents. Loving adults who would be delighted to hug, express affection, pat a shoulder for encouragement, or hold a hand for friendship are forbidden to meet this great need. I wonder how many problem children in the public schools would be dramatically improved if they were hugged as well as taught?

We also need to be touched for our mental and emotion ~al health. We are beings whose emotional, mental, and physical attributes are integrated. A lack of contact in any of these areas will effect our well-being, our health. As the authorities searched for the "unibomber" in the mid-1990s there was speculation about what kind of a profile the man who sent death through the mail might have. It was suggested by many on the news-talk television shows that in all likelihood he was a loner who had isolated himself. When Ted Kazinsky was finally located and arrested in 1995, that was exactly what the authorities discovered. He lived in a cabin miles from other people. In his isolation he was being touched by no-one, and his mental health was certainly not enhanced by it!

John McCain (imprisoned in Vietnam, 1967-1973) and other prisoners of war of have shared how profound an impact isolation had on them. Men in this sort of circumstance come up with all sorts of elaborate ways to contact one another. By tapping on walls with Morse code, writing notes on toilet paper, whispering in the dark, contact is attempted by whatever means can be devised. It's a lifeline for hope. It seems no accident to me that people who are released from this sort of isolated captivity are inevitably shown hugging whoever sets them free.

How Does Touch Affect People?

There are a lot of benefits that can result from a loving touch. The **embrace** can be an expression of forgiveness. Those who come into contact with a Christian who knows about a past sin can feel intimated and indicted, even if the Christian has never said a condemning word. However, when the Christian friend embraces them, the acceptance and forgiveness that is conveyed is profound. How can we withhold the forgiveness that Christ has extended to us? Which of us is without sin of our own and hasn't needed forgiveness?

"Be kind and compassionate to one another,
forgiving each other, just as in Christ God forgave you."
Ephesians 4:32

It can also be a **covering** of righteousness - love and right relationship passed on. The embrace is by its very nature an intimate gesture. We have to be willing to open our arms and draw another in close to our chest, near our heart. A real embrace can't be done at arms length. The gesture of drawing someone in close is truly an imitation of what Christ does for us. Righteousness is right relationship with God, and an embrace emulates it by offering a right relationship one to another.

"...Love covers a multitude of sins." 1 Peter 4: 8

The touch of blessing frees people from the past as the **grip** of guilt is loosened. What is being offered is true freedom.

The **handclasp** of fellowship is also a form of blessing touch. When we extend our hand in accepting welcome, there is a bond, an intimacy, that is confirmed. It not only welcomes, it includes. It blesses.

Do watch out for cultural sensitivities in the realm of touch. For example, in the Fresno area, we have a large Hmong community, the Southeast Asian people from the hill county of Laos. It is taboo to touch a child on the head because they believe it allows the entrance of demons. Some Asians, like the Japanese, are very formal and might think a hug is improper.

In addition, some who have been physically abused are very reluctant to respond positively to a hug. Whether it is a cultural or personal reticence, it is usually acceptable to extend a hand for a handshake. It order to make it warmer, I have occasionally held the hand a bit longer than would usually be the case, even sometimes putting my other had on top to convey more connection. Allow the Holy Spirit to make you sensitive to what is going to be appropriate.

While physical touch is our primary method of connection in the blessing, touching by means of the telephone or in writing can also have great, positive impact. These two means are certainly concrete and positive. The day before Lisa's memorial service a got a phone call from Pastor Johnson. He said that he had called in to the office that morning and learned Lisa had passed on. He was very affirming, saying kind and encouraging things, including how important we were to the church and how he was praying for us. It was so meaningful to me. I thanked him, and added that I was surprised to hear from him because I thought he was still in Korea at a conference. I asked where he was calling from and he replied, "Seoul." Believe me, I felt valued and blest!

Carefully chosen cards can have a similar effect. As I got up on a morning I was leaving for a speaking engagement, I realized Noel had already left for work. I found he had left me a note with this blessing:

Traveling mercies,
Speaking blessings
And may the Lord cover you,
His Spirit fill you,
And give you many victories and peace.
Love, Noel

Going through some old letters, I came across a birthday letter my mom sent in 1981. I'd saved it because of the blessing she wrote.

"As your birthday approaches, we want to take the opportunity to express our pride and joy in you. We rejoice that you chose a Christian man and are raising you little family in Sunday School and church.

We know the Lord has something special to do through you as you came very close to dying your first year. We gave you up to God at that time. He could have taken you if He had not some good plan for you.

Our love always, Mom and Dad."

Blessings committed to paper can be tangible treasures that touch again and again.   Mom is gone on, but I felt her loving hug once more.

The Laying on of Hugs

I have often thought that one of the ordinances of the church should be the *Laying on of Hugs*. Some have had way too little practice at, it so now is your chance to get some. Stand up and go find some to hug! Practice makes perfect.

Do a personal inventory on your experience as you practice hugging.

How does it make you feel?
What changes in your attitude are you able to discern?
What effect does it have on the people you hug?
What changes in expression on their faces do you notice?
Do they noticeably relax? Warm up to you?
Do they seem grateful for the gesture?
Take note of anything you become aware of.
Enjoy yourself!

"I have loved you with an everlasting love..."

Jeremiah 31:3a

Chapter Six
PERSONAL AFFIRMATION

KEY TERMS

Expressing
Making something known by words and actions.

Perspective
A point of view; a particular way of looking at something.

Valuation
The considered worth of something.

Paradigm
A working model; a pattern; an example.

KEY QUESTIONS

❖ What constitutes a clear view of things?
❖ What do eyes of love see?
❖ What is God's perspective?
❖ What does love cost?
❖ What's the guaranty?
❖ Am I worthy? Strong enough? Wise enough?
❖ What's wrong with my old paradigm?

The Motivation of Love

Let me ask you a question:
What constitutes a clear view of things?
Did you ever wonder what God saw in the beginning?
When He considered each aspect of His creation one by one,
what He saw was perfection.

*"And God saw that it was good(v5)." "God saw all that He had
made, and it was very good."* Genesis 1:, Genesis 1: 31

As the Alpha and Omega, He knows the beginning
and the end. God sees what should have been. I wonder
how often we catch a glimpse of that? God knew what the
consequences of sin would be, although we all too often seem
oblivious to them. It never ceases to amaze me the things
people will do that are just bound to have consequences I
know they won't like. From skipping homework to lying to
your boss, things have a way of coming out. When Noel was in
the Air Force, we had only one car. We lived in a small house
that took little time to clean. I really didn't have a lot to do,
but we were expecting a baby so I didn't pursue a job that I
would have soon left. So, on the days I didn't have the car, I'd
do what little needed to be done, then I'd have time on my
hands. I fell into the habit of watching a particular soap opera
each day. One day I found myself talking out loud to one of
the characters on the show! The silly woman was about to have
an affair with her best friend's husband, and I told her, "Don't
you know that you'll destroy your friendship, your marriage
and hers, and you'll probably end up having an illegitimate
baby, to boot! She wasn't giving any thought at all to what

119

the consequences of her act would be! (Then it occurred to me that I was talking to the TV! Oh, fine . . . I'm talking to a fictional character that I've begun to think of as a friend. I'm acting as stupidly as she is! I found other things to do with my time.)

I want you to take a few moments and list sins and their consequences that you can think of or that the Holy Spirit identifies for you. Now jot down what comes to mind.

Sins	Consequences

What did you put on your list?

❖ Did you put down lying?   When the truth comes out, as it always does eventually, the consequences will certainly make the liar look bad (or worse!)

    If I lie in court, the consequence of such perjury is jail!

    If I lie in the workplace, attempting to excuse myself, I may well lose my job.

    If I lie in a personal situation to build myself up at the expense of another, I'll lose friends.

❖ What about stealing?   I could go to jail, or at least humiliated.

❖ If I cheat, I could have the same consequences as lying.

❖ Another form of cheating is adultery and its consequence is loss of trust and perhaps the loss of my marriage.

❖ Gossip is easy to do, but it can destroy someone's reputation and shatter friendships.

❖ Disobedience or rebellion toward God has several possible consequences, all of them awful.

    Growth that God intends for me could be blocked.

    There will probably be lost opportunity.

    It could diminish my ability to hear from God next time.

    There could be people who didn't hear God's message because I didn't speak when I should have.

In contrast to the sin that is so often easily seen (and looked for), **what do eyes of love see?** God not only sees what the consequences of sin will be, He sees the potential for good as clearly. His eyes of love see what I can be, the possibilities and potentials of each life.

121

How do you see yourself right now? Is your self view any different than before you knew Christ? Than last year?

Think honestly, looking backward. Can you see change and growth? If we take larger chunks of time, it should be possible to spot them. If we can't see any growth or positive changes in our lives over time, we need to do serious business with the Lord about not walking in obedience, because the scriptural pattern is that we are being perfected (that is matured) day by day.

If someone asked you to describe how you think God sees you, what would you say? If I was there with you, what would you tell me? Be honest with yourself. I'm not there for you to feel embarrassed! Did your honest answer surprise you? If you were to ask folks in your church group, you might very well find that those who were raised in the church would give you a response that sounds like the result of **rote learning**. Perhaps something like, "God loves me and has a wonderful plan for my life." That's probably what I would have answered when I was a college student active in Campus Crusade for Christ, and for years afterward.

Don't get me wrong, it's a correct answer; it's just that I've had the feeling that this response might be more from head knowledge than heart knowledge.

Newer Christians may very well say something like, "God probably thinks I never do anything right," or "God is probably disappointed in me," or "I know God loves me but he probably doesn't think much of how I'm doing. I'll never be Billy Graham!" Actually, nobody but Billy himself will ever be Billy Graham!

In what ways can a person's view of himself differ from God's view of him? Pause and consider a moment. Let me suggest some:

❖ God sees what *can* be as well as what *is.*
His view is not restricted to our limitations of time or space, our abilities or our understanding.

❖ No sin is too great to forgive.
Anyone can be forgiven, even those who have committed the most heinous crimes.

❖ God doesn't just repair, He re-creates.
Wow! What an amazing thought! Frontward or backward, that's still a Wow! It's not God's purpose to patch lives, or put Band-Aids on wounds. He makes us new creations in Christ. (2 Corinthians 5:17)

If you have trouble seeing as God sees, then perhaps this should be your cry. Help! I need new glasses! I am most decidedly not seeing things as God sees them!

To make new glasses, you don't start with lens grinding. First, you have to have an eye exam by someone who is qualified. Spiritually speaking, the Great Physician is the only one accepted by our HMO, Heaven's Medical Organization! You can't use your old prescription, either, if you want to see more clearly.

During the exam the doctor will check to see if there is anything blocking the vision: spiritual cataracts, disobedience or disbelief. He'll also check for filters, kind of like shades, that shouldn't be there, including un-biblical teachings or misunderstandings.

What will the result of your new lenses? The most important thing is that there is great freedom in the clarity they provide because you will be able to see what God sees, the truth.

"Jesus said, 'If you hold to my teaching, you are really my disciples. Then you will know the truth, and the truth will set you free.'" John 8:31b-32

What is God's perspective?

God is our Abba Father, our dad. He doesn't want to be a distant, cold, terror-inspiring dictator. While He wants an intimate relationship with us, He does have the advantage of having the view from heaven, standing outside of time.

When He looks over the portals of glory, God sees history from the top down: He sees it all at the same time.

Because we're beings who are created in time, it's hard for us to see the overview. We can't readily stand outside our selves, let alone outside of the time that frames us. In high school, when my friends and I wanted to be sarcastic (which was most of the time, I'm sorry to admit) we had a particularly useful quip. "You have a profound grasp of . . . the obvious! Hindsight is perfect for the *obvious* reason that it happened already! History can tell us what we need to know about what is going on around us only with the distance of time. But take another look at that word, history. If you think of it as *His story*, overview becomes possible now rather than later. He knows the future as well as He knows the past, and we can trust what He tells us about what is going on. When He declares something is possible, we can believe Him!

We know that God places high value on people because 1 Timothy 2:4 tells us that God "*... wants all men to be saved and to come to a knowledge of the truth.*" He values people so highly that he wants **all** of them to be saved. He always has. Jesus' life, death and resurrection is the clear

124

demonstration of that central truth. God doesn't stop there, though. He not only provides for our eternity, He cares about our present and all the days we have to spend before eternity begins in our new tent. He has wonderful plans for us here and now.

"For I know the plans I have for you," declares the LORD, "plans to prosper you and not to harm you, plans to give you a hope and a future." Jeremiah 29:11

Can we get a glimpse of what God sees, of the plans that He is laying out? Absolutely! I see evidence everywhere I look.

Over the years I've learned to see God at work all around me, and I long ago realized there is no such thing as luck. There's no such thing as coincidence. Many of you, like me, could tell story after story of how God has orchestrated events to bless, to teach, to comfort, to protect, to give a hope and a future, and so much more.

One of the most vivid views of God's careful planning I've ever witnessed occurred in our church sanctuary. It was near the conclusion of a special Sunday morning worship service. Don Moen was our special guest that morning as our choir helped him premier his musical work, "God For Us." Debbie, a friend of mine, had her parents visiting and they went with her and her family to the incredible worship service we had at church that morning. The anointing was so heavy that in the choir loft we found it hard to remain standing and sing at times. I've never experienced such a spirit of worship. As the service was nearing its conclusion and the time to offer an opportunity for people to accept Christ was approaching, my friend's mom slipped out to go to the restroom. Rather than disturb the service at such a crucial time, she went out to wait in the car.

Debbie's dad, a quiet and reserved man, was deeply touched by the Spirit during worship. Rather to her surprise, he raised his hands in unselfconscious praise for the first time. It was her last memory of his life. While she focused on the worship herself, he slumped to the floor with a heart attack and was gone. The Lord had orchestrated her dad's home-going so that his last moments were spent in a new breakthrough of praise. Her last vision of him was of that wonderful moment in his life, and her mom was spared the agony of seeing the futile effort to revive him. Like my friend Debbie said, "it was a God thing."

Watching Jesus

Looking at Jesus and through him seeing the Father, our natural response is worship for the incredible love of God. We've talked about the fact that love is an intellectual decision, but it is also true that where the mind leads, the heart follows. Music is the expression of the heart, and worship has always expressed itself in music.

When we sing and express our love in worship, we sense God's love for us. In a manner of speaking, our worship becomes a duet of love. What Jesus wanted was for us to be able to sing along!

So, it was that desire that bound Jesus to the cross. He was handcuffed by his love for us. Our music lessons were expensive!

There are so many wonderful songs about Jesus' love for us and the incredible price He paid us on the cross. Darlene Zscheh is the worship leader of a huge church in Australia. She has a rare gift for expressing the love and thanks we feel toward Him. One of the worship songs she wrote is a new setting of an old, old theme.

Worthy is the Lamb [14]

Thank You for the cross, Lord.
Thank You for the price You paid.
Bearing all my sin and shame,
In love You came and gave amazing grace.
Thank You for this love, Lord.
Thank You for the nail pierced hands.
Wash me in Your cleansing flow,
Now all I know,
Your forgiveness and embrace.

The chorus declares, "Worthy is the Lamb." He is worthy indeed. Did you notice where the verse concludes? All that Jesus accomplished on the cross He offers through His embrace. A song by Charles H. Gabriel[15] completes the thought.

He Lifted Me

His brow was pierced with many a thorn,
His hands by cruel nails were torn,
When from my guilt and grief forlorn,
In love He lifted me.
From sinking sand He lifted me,
With tender hand He lifted ...

In order for us to see from God's perspective, we need to have a shift in our sodality and paradigms. Let's look at those two things and see how that might help us.

Sodality and Paradigm: one, two, three, shift!

Sodality is a way of viewing something. For instance, an architect's blueprint for viewing a house is an example of a sodality.

It might help you to understand if you think of yourself as in the center of a series of circles. In the first ring outside yourself would be your immediate family and closest friends. In the next you would place your extended family. In the next ring is your community, then your region or state, your country, and finally your world farthest out. These circles are sodalities that frame your point of view, how you see things. The most important is your internal, personal view point. Your immediate family and closest friends add new dimensions to the sodality. Each frame of reference has its effect.

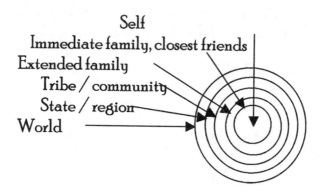

Self
Immediate family, closest friends
Extended family
Tribe / community
State / region
World

A paradigm is a working model or example that serves

as a pattern or a mold. The 5 parts of the biblical model act as a paradigm for extending blessing.

It isn't native to us to see from God's perspective, to use a sodality that is in sync with His. Our natural sodality is rooted in our own experience, knowledge, and understanding. It is inherently limited by our inability to see an adequate overview. Our perspective is too narrow and sketchy to be of great use to the kingdom. In our native sodality we're inclined to see sin and failure, not forgiveness and potential. We have difficulty seeing a person valued by God who can be re-created by Him. In our fallen / natural sodality, we see the past relatively well, but the future poorly, if at all.

We must strive to shift our sodality and paradigms to come into alignment with God's. We need to work to see according to His sodality, from His perspective, because it doesn't happen without effort and purpose on our part. Let me encourage you. I grew up with a mom who was famous in our extended family for seeing *everything* God's way (or so it seemed to us!) To tell you the truth, it drove me crazy as a kid! To every flippant remark she would reply, "Do you think that's really the way God would have you talk?" Television shows that had something unscriptural were *always* remarked on. She even wrote notes in the margins of books she read if they strayed from the Truth! When I complained about a geometry teacher who was unfair to me, she asked, "Have you been praying for him?" No... (I found out later she did write him a sweet note reminding him of his responsibility as a teacher to his students. He actually answered my questions after that, and in a cordial way, besides!) At her memorial service, one of the cousins started us all chuckling when he recalled that when one of us was in for a "God reminder" she would begin with, "Now Dearie..." With consistent effort and practice, it does become more automatic and instinctive. I know...I do the same things to my kids!

Then, we must use His pattern and model, Jesus, for how we live and operate.

Jesus paid the full price for us to be able to shift sodalities and implement a new paradigm, a new pattern for blessing. It's worthwhile to remind ourselves what paying the full price actually meant now and then.

Paying the Full Price

What does love cost? For Jesus, the answer was everything.

"Jesus commanded Peter, "Put your sword away! Shall I not drink the cup the Father has given me?" John 18:11

He drank the whole cup. It cost the Father, too:

"This is how God showed his love among us: He sent his one and only Son into the world that we might live through him. This is love: not that we loved God, but that he loved us and sent his Son as an atoning sacrifice for our sins." 1 John 4:9-10

When I first took Evangelism Explosion,[16] a witnessing training program by Dr. D. James Kennedy, I already knew the famous two questions the program teaches you to use. In fact, I had been wanting to take the course for years and had not been able to squeeze it into a packed schedule. When the

Lord opened the way, I was delighted and I finally learned what went with the two questions!

❖ Have you come to the place in your spiritual life where you know for certain that if you were to die today you would go to heaven?

❖ Suppose you were to die today and stand before God, and He were to ask you "Why should I let you in to my heaven?" what would you say?

The person being asked these questions who expresses interest but doesn't know the biblical answers has an opportunity then to hear the basic gospel message. The explanation of the gospel is elegant in its simplicity, with 5 clear points.

1. By His grace, God offers us heaven / eternal life as a free gift because it can be neither earned or deserved.

2. We are sinners and all we deserve is death.

3. God loves us and wants to be merciful to us. However, He is also just and must punish sin.

4. He solved our dilemma through His son Jesus, the perfect, infinite God-man who took the penalty on Himself. He died and rose from the dead, paying the penalty for our sin and purchasing a place in heaven for us.

5. We can receive this free gift through faith.

I think that we sometimes forget what good news this really is!

Most of us can answer the two questions with "Yes, I'm certain I have eternal life." And, "I would say to God, 'You should let me in because I have accepted Jesus as my Savior and Lord.' We understand that Jesus' sacrifice bought deliverance from sin with its penalty of death. What we often don't emphasize enough is that this deliverance means being crucified with Christ.

 Excuse me? What's that mean? We aren't just delivered *from* our sin, we're delivered *to* a new life. We have to understand that the old existence is dead, crucified with Christ. Way too many Christians have old nature zombies up walking around. No wonder their lives stink!

Galatians 2:20 lays out for us the truth that when we have been crucified with Christ it should be that it is no longer we who live, but *Christ who lives in us.* The life we live in the body, we must live by faith in the Son of God, who loved us and gave himself for us.

We need to bury those old bodies and quit digging them up! We realize that our deliverance / salvation was possible because He took our sins on Himself. Recorded centuries ahead of time, Isaiah wrote in chapter 53: 5-6b that our sin was literally put on him. The punishment that brought us peace was upon him, and by his wounds we are healed. He said it so plainly.

But, it's also important to remember that He took *our sin nature* on Himself as well. Paul points out in Romans 6:6-7 that we know that our old self was crucified with Him so that our old nature might be done away with so that we would no longer be slaves to sin. Unless we die to sin we can never be free from its bondage and power. That's exactly what happens for us as we make Jesus not only our Savior but our Lord, holding back nothing of our old self.

132

Best of all, God has given us a guaranty that our old nature has been defeated. The Holy Spirit seals us or puts His mark on us when we believe and receive Christ. As Ephesians 1:13b-14 puts it, *"He is Himself a deposit guaranteeing our inheritance until the redemption of those who are God's possession – to the praise of his glory."*

Since Jesus paid the full price for sin because of His great love for us, it clearly follows that we are precious to Him and highly valued. The enemy doesn't want us to really grasp this truth. He values me and you, and everyone else!

1. Jot down 3 things that repeatedly try to spring up out of your old nature:

2. Insert them one at a time into the following prayer:

Lord, I send _____ to the cross and accept that it died there, having lost its legitimate power over me forever.

As Christians, part of our job is to help people accept God's valuation of them. We need to make sure we have done the same ourselves. Take a few moments to do this exercise. When I did it, I found I could think of more than three things! As we try to help people understand God's valuation of them, what are some of the questions that come up?

Accepting God's Valuation

There are a number of questions that swirl around at the core of the personal valuation issue and they provide a good lens for looking at it.

"Am I worthy?"
Self Esteem versus God's Esteem

While they may not voice it out loud, many people struggle with the question "Am I worthy?" The issue here is their self esteem. Do you remember what God said in the first chapter of Genesis when He made man? He said that He (actually He said 'us,' indicating the Trinity) made man in His ('our') image and likeness. Then, when He had accomplished that incredible thing, He added that He looked carefully at what He had done and declared that it was . . . junk? Just o. k.? Passable? Simply acceptable? No way. He said His work was good. Who are we to argue with Him about it? Don't mistake me. I don't mean we don't need saving; we do. Adam and Eve took care of that in the garden (they don't get a *thank you very much* for that one!) But it does mean that God put His own stamp on man and consequently we are infinitely valuable. I love the passage in Matthew 10:29-31 where Jesus talks about the sparrows. They can be pesky nuisances, but ...

"Are not two sparrows sold for a penny? Yet not one of them will fall to the ground apart from the will of your Father. And the very hairs of your head are all numbered. So don't be afraid; **you are worth more than many sparrows.***"*

Scripture clearly teaches God thinks we are worthy of His esteem, and He always acts on what He thinks.

"Am strong enough?"
Our Strength versus God's Strength

One of the first realities new Christians face is that meeting God's expectations isn't hard. It's impossible ...unless He helps us. Are we strong enough? **No, but Christ is.**

"But he said to me,
'My grace is sufficient for you,
for my power is made perfect in **weakness.***'*
Therefore I will boast all the more gladly about my weakness,
so that Christ's power may rest on me.

That is why, for Christ's sake, I delight in weakness, in insults, in hardships, in persecutions, in difficulties. For when I am weak, then I am strong." Corinthians 12: 9-10

"Am I wise enough?"
Our word versus God's Word

"Jesus answered, 'It is written, 'Man does not live on bread alone, but on every word that comes from the mouth of God.'"
Matthew 4: 4

The Apostle Peter was stating the absolute truth when he answered Jesus in John 6: 68. Who else can we go to for the wisdom we need? He is the one with the words of eternal life.

We have to be fully persuaded ourselves, then live out these truths in what we teach, what we do, and what we say so that these truths are evident:

❖ People are worthy and valuable to God.
❖ **In Christ** we are all more than able – we're strong.
❖ And God delights in giving wisdom as we put on the mind of Christ through the Word and listen as the Spirit brings the Word to life.

We talked about the importance of shifting to God's perspective and using His pattern, and I'm sure you realize this can require an attitude adjustment on our part. One of the things we need to shift attitudes about is our concept of what is natural.

Unnatural or supernatural natural results are really what we need to be looking for. What God created in the beginning is what is actually natural. We live in a fallen world in which what we generally consider natural or normal isn't *God's natural*. Shift your sodality – we need to go by God's blueprint, not the world's.

What else is required in shifting to God's perspective? We have to move our acceptance of the unconditional high value of people out of the realm of theory and put it into practice.

I am certain that none of you would say that you believe some people are inherently more valuable than others. But, how often has someone in one our groups sat alone and no one joined her, or a new person been left to fend for herself? If we really value the people around us, do we take our shepherding responsibility seriously?

Does *anyone notice* if a particular person stops coming? Are all the regular attenders being observed by someone in leadership so that gifts can be identified and encouraged? If you are a leader, this should be part of your job description. Do you know what their gifts are? Strengths? Weaknesses, so that difficulties can be headed off at the pass? Are you observing them enough so that you can see what their needs are?

For those of us in leadership, too often we are so concerned about running our programs that we forget that our real job is *shepherding* people, reaching out and connecting with them. For those of you who aren't officially in leadership or you don't have a specific job right now, remember we are all ministers. You can spot a person sitting alone as easily as your leader, and it may be a great deal easier for you to go sit next to her! For those who are older, it also means there is no such thing as spiritual retirement. Do we really value people like the Lord does? To do that requires an action attitude.

What's an action attitude? We know from James 2:17 that faith without actions (works) is dead. I would suggest to you that attitude without actions is also dead.

Faith without actions =̲ attitude without actions.

137

If we actually have the right attitude, our actions will demonstrate it. If we honestly look at how we spend our ministry time, how we conduct our ministries in the larger sense as well as ministry in the personal, and have to admit it doesn't reflect a shepherd's heart for the sheep, we need to do business with that.

Our ministries shouldn't have sheep that are getting lost or hurt and getting left behind.

For way too many of us way too much of the time, there is a credibility gap between how we say we value people and how we actually conduct our ministries. Our first commitment has got to be shepherding the people who have been entrusted into our care and really see them.

One of the best most basic actions for showing a right attitude is affirmation. Affirm, affirm, affirm. It is virtually impossible to affirm too much. It goes a long way toward breaking the block of feeling unloved.

How Do You Affirm?

❖ Use names

Our son, Tyler, didn't like his name when he was growing up. In high school he decided 'Ty' wasn't too bad, but *nobody* was named Tyler. Ugh. My, how times have changed! But whether we like our name or not, it is an integral part of our identity. One of the department stores I shop in has an employee named Teresa who is sometimes called over the loudspeaker. *I know* I don't work there, and no one who knows me would realize I'm in the store, but every time it happens I turn around like as if they're calling me! There's

138

just something about one's own name. I don't think that's much of a surprise when I consider how big a deal God makes about His name.

There's nothing that establishes connection between people faster or more positively than using names. Use names and memorize them as quickly as possible. Work at it! I have a lot of empathy for those of you who struggle with remembering names, but if I can improve at it, anyone can! When I meet people for the first time I often say something like, "I kind of struggle with names, so if I can't remember yours right off, please don't be insulted if I ask again. I really want to remember. When I get to heaven, I'm going to be like pastor!" That always gets a laugh, because he's famous in our congregation for his memory for names.

Pastor Johnson has the most amazing memory for names I've ever seen. If he's met you once, it's *very* likely he'll remember your name. He knows most of the people who are regular attendees of our church by name (I don't know how many that is exactly, but out of 5000 adults and children, it could be as many as 1000 people, and that doesn't include all those he knows beyond our congregation! I may not become a G. L. Johnson in the name department, but I can certainly work at it!

When Tyler was interviewing for the position of senior pastor of a church in our region, he told me that his plan was to write down and memorize the names of everyone he met at the church. He kept a little notebook in his pocket, and as soon as possible he wrote the names down. Before each visit, he'd review the names of those he had met so far. After he was installed as the new pastor, people were amazed and delighted to discover that he already knew the names of all the people in the congregation he had met during the interviewing process! It made an instantaneously strong bond that has helped him quickly become established in his congregation so he could move ahead with the work the Lord has called him there to do.

❖ Give full attention. When my granddaughter, Katie, was small she already understood how important this is. If she didn't get your full attention, she would take your face in her little hands and turn it toward her!

Sometimes I feel like doing that, too! Like when I was chatting with an acquaintance in the hallway at church recently who kept looking around at everyone who was passing by. Perhaps you've had that experience, too. Believe me, it didn't make me feel like she was interested in our conversation, or worse, in me. Maybe you can identify.

Eye contact is essential to good communication and it's how you telegraph your interest and attention. My cousin, Nancy, is the reigning queen of attentive listening. When we were kids she was a favorite cousin, but not just for me. Everyone in the family loved her. As an adult, I got to thinking about her one day, about how universally loved she was. What was it about her that caused us all to feel that way? Her face came to mind and I had a very clear image of it, much more so than most other people, though I didn't really see her frequently. I realized suddenly that when she talked to me her eyes never left my face, that she gave her full and complete attention. Her image was clear in my mind because we had more eye contact! It was her habit with everyone.

Giving full attention communicates several things:

140

You are important to me.

I really want to hear what you have to say.

Other things can wait. You are a priority.

…No wonder everyone loves Nancy.

❖ Value presence. Notice the people around you, who is at church and who isn't. If you are in leadership and your church or group doesn't have a system for keeping track and following up by cards or phone calls or some such, start one. You can call or send a note on your own, too. This isn't my strongest suit, but I have to admit I love it when someone does it for me. This is something *I'm* working on.

Camelia Cross leads the Evangelism Explosion program in our church. She is the most consistent about valuing presence I've ever seen. You get a card from her *every* time you're absent from E. E.! She has an upbeat card ready for each in the group to sign with a short note and mails it out after the meeting you missed so you get it immediately. You *know* they missed you and value your presence. Camelia is also terrific at valuing what people do, and thanking them for it.

❖ Value participation and effort. It's pretty hard to be thanked too much! I love Camelia's cards. They brighten my day and let me know what I *do is noticed and appreciated.* Most of us aren't thanked enough … Take time to notice what people do and comment on what you see; encourage and thank them.

Noel told me of a conversation he had with a friend just today that shows how much it means to value what people do. His friend, Rudy, mentioned that he put in a lot of time and effort supporting the Rescue Mission, but no

141

seemed to care particularly, nor say thanks. Then, he told Noel a story that obviously moved Rudy deeply. He said that last week-end the West Coast Regional Director and the International Director of the Rescue Mission organization were in town to meet with the local workers and supporters. Rudy felt the Lord prompting him to lead the local folks in prayer to affirm these visiting leaders. He ushered the group into a room where they could pray, and explained to the gathering that he wanted the local group to pray a blessing over these dedicated men and their wives, to affirm them. They went to prayer, and as Christians usually do, prayed for God to provide for the ministry, meet the needs for staff, support, and so on. Finally, Rudy stopped them and kindly said, "No, you don't understand. I want us *to affirm them, to thank them.* I want us to *bless them.* He had them go back to prayer, but this time he prayed as he knew God was leading him.

The men and women broke down and cried as they understood the power of what was happening. *They were all blessed.* Afterward, the directors shared that no one had ever blessed them before... They were more grateful than they could say.   Noel's friend is still waiting for his co-laborers to bless *him.* We can step in and fill the void of thanks and blessing if only we will.

❖ Notice appearance— is it notable in some *positive* way? Is there something different about it, something that has changed for the better?   Say so! It only takes a moment and it means so much. There is *always some attribute* you can praise. Is she bright and insightful? Say so. Is he wearing a great tie? Is the color she's wearing especially flattering?   Be observant; purpose to pay attention.

142

This is not a skill that is native to all of us. Some analytical, detail oriented people pick up on things around them without trying, but the rest of us have to *purpose to see.* You'll be amazed at how delighted people are that you noticed they lost weight, or have a new hair style, or look especially sharp. Everyone wants to be noticed like that, even the shy ones. I have never yet had someone respond, "You have a lot of nerve noticing I'm wearing a flattering outfit!" But I have had *lots* of people respond in a very surprised way, and positively light up. Then smiling from head to toe say something like, "You think so? Gee, thanks…"

Avoid the temptation of becoming so caught up in what you have to get done or working to see that some event or program goes smoothly, that you stop seeing the people who come. Ministry isn't about program, it's about people!

❖ Notice expressions and take note of body language, and respond! We all know a great deal about what unspoken communication says, but we don't necessarily take the time to notice and respond to it. Don't let yourself get carried away in the realm of body language, but do pay attention.

Not everyone has so dramatic a sad-sack slump when things aren't going well as my grandson, Jacob, but everyone sends messages non-verbally.

❖ Purpose to affirm your children by blessing them on a regular basis. Daily probably isn't too often! I love the tradition of the conservative Jewish households in which the father blesses the children at the Friday evening

Sabbath dinner. Blessing your little ones can help build a hedge around them of your love and God's love for them. A hedge of blessing benefits any child, whether he is in daycare, from a divorced home, or just facing the normal trials of growing up. Using the blessing with our children can safeguard their emotional health so that when they are older they can receive the ministry and plan God has for them.

Before a child leaves for school or as they are going to sleep for the night are good times for a short blessing. It doesn't have to be long, and it's more power – full if you insert their names into scripture. For example, as your child leaves for school and you hug him good-by, you can say something like, "The Lord bless and keep you, today, Ben. I know the Lord has a good plan for you today, and as you study and do your best, you'll be a workman the Lord approves. Remember, Ben, the Lord will help you today, and so will I." That little blessing included words from Numbers 6:24, Jer. 29:11, 2 Tim. 2:15, and Ps. 121:1.

❖ Most of all, value people. Take mental notes about the people who populate your sphere of influence. Is someone doing something particularly worth while like working as a volunteer at your local hospice, writing a book, or taking care of foster children? When you learn of it, you can ask about it again later and it will bless them. Are you inclined to have a bad memory? Write things down! Re-inquire if you can't remember.

❖ Ask the Lord to help you value people:
To give you ever growing love for them.
To give you an encouragement for them.

To give you a verse for them, then jot it down and say when you see them next.

Who can you think of that needs affirming, who needs to know that they are valued and valuable?   What are you going to do about it? Be specific.

"The tongue

has

the power

of

life
and
death"

Proverbs 18:21a

Chapter Seven
PARTICULAR LANGUAGE

KEY TERMS

Verbalization
Speaking out something; putting into spoken words.

Nurture
To raise or bring up; to nourish or rear.

Prerequisite
That which is required in advance of something.

Potential
That which is possible, could be developed or used.

Methodology
An orderly body of methods or procedures; an orderly way of doing something.

KEY QUESTIONS

- ❖ How does God activate His will?
- ❖ What's the relationship of words, faith and power?
- ❖ What are the potentials in words?
- ❖ What is a verbal grace gift?
- ❖ How can we bless the Lord?
- ❖ How can we receive blessing?
- ❖ How can we pass on blessing?

The Power in Words

It's been a lot of years since the day in kindergarten when Angie told me my long, ringlet-curls were full of something that should be flushed. I still remember the sting of the hurt and embarrassment. Like other kids, I chanted the rhyme "sticks and stones can break my bones, but words can never hurt me." We all learned that that's not necessarily so. Words can easily become sticks and stones that cause deep and lasting hurt. But we also learned that just like sticks and stones, words can be building materials.

The question we need to deal with is whether the sticks and stones of *our words* are going to be bone breakers or building blocks.

Let me ask you: How does God activate His will? God has a methodology that is fascinating and important for us. The first place we see it in operation is in creation. John 1 tells us that the Word was in the beginning. Psalm 33:6 adds that it was by the Word of the LORD that the heavens were made. Even the multitudes of stars were made by the breath of His mouth, it says. It is in verbalization that God releases His creative power.

> *"For He spoke, and it came to be;*
> *He commanded, and it stood firm."* Psalm 33:9

There are so many places in scripture where you find the phrase *and God Said* or find the scripture quoting

149

something He said as a means of releasing His power. Genesis Chapter one over and over shows the link between what God said and the power that was released.

"Let there be"
"And God said, 'Let there be light.
...Let there be an expanse between the waters
to separate water from water.
...And it was so.'
...Let there be ...let there be...
...And it was so."

Genesis 1:2 teaches that the words themselves were the power because it was truly creation here – something was being brought out of nothing: because it takes note of the fact that the earth was a formless void.

What's the explanation for what's going on here? It's really clear in Isaiah 46:11b and 55:11. God says that what He *says* He will bring about. Then He goes further and says that what He has planned is exactly what He will do.

His declaration and promise is that what goes out from his mouth – His Word – will not return to Him empty, or uncompleted. Rather it will accomplish what He desires and achieve the purpose for which He sent it.

There is power in God's words. There is also power in our words because we are made in God's image. James 3 teaches about the awesome power of what we say along with many other scriptures, but it is best summed up in Proverbs 18:21:

There is life and death in the power of the tongue.

When we consider the kinds of words we are inclined to speak, we find so often they come out wrong. Too many times I've cringed and though, "Did I really say that?" We know from Proverbs 12:18 and from experience that reckless words really can pierce like a sword, and the tongue of the wise actually does bring healing.

We try to guard our words because we know the truth of *Proverbs 13:3* that if we guard our lips, what we're really doing is guarding our life. This is because if we speak rashly we can easily come to ruin.

The problem is, of course, we are inclined to fail at this lip guarding business, and end up saying something we shouldn't. Then, like the prophet in Isaiah 6:5 be forced to cry,

"Woe to me!"
"...I am ruined!
For I am a man (woman) of unclean lips ..."

Remember what I said about my mom? Well, she wasn't *really* a wet blanket ... honest! Actually, she was quite darling. I asked her once how she managed to keep such a tight reign of her mouth? She never seemed to say anything she regretted. Her answer was wonderful.

"When I was a child in Sunday school," she said, "one day the teacher talked about the words to a song we sang, 'Be careful little mouth what you say.' On the wall of the classroom was a picture of a Roman soldier she had used to teach about the armor of God. I got to thinking about that soldier and it occurred to me that I could post guards like that on my mouth. So I asked Jesus to station one on each side, and whenever I started to say something I shouldn't, they

151

could cross their spears and it wouldn't come out! They're still at their posts."

What's the solution, then? Do we need to post tiny guards? It might not be a bad idea, but the underlying idea here is that we make it our desire to have the words of our mouths be consistent with God's Word.

Just think of what can be accomplished for good if we connect our power to God's far greater power.

I've tried to illustrate this concept for you in the following power formula:

$$S^2 F = E = M C^2$$

Most of us marginal science types may not be able to explain Einstein's equation $E = MC^2$ very completely, but I do know that:

- $\triangleright$ E stands for Energy,
- $\triangleright$ M stands for Mass or Matter,
- $\triangleright$ C stands for the speed of light squared

It occurred to me that we can plug in S^2F and have it = E (energy, power.) In this new equation,

- $\triangleright$ F stands for faith
- $\triangleright$ S is the force of speech squared by the Word as the accelerator

When we bring what we say into agreement with what God says there is multiplied power released. You might say to yourself, boy is that a stretch, but think about it. Jesus said, that He is the light of the world in John 8:12. In this equation, it's the speed of light multiplied by that which is matter or has weight, mass. Hebrews 11:1 is revealing when

152

it tells us that faith is the *substance* of the things we hope for. Substance, as in matter or mass!

As Jesus is the light, He is also the Word. 'C' stands for the speed of light. A word spoken is a thought put into motion. Isn't it interesting that the letter 'C' stands for the speed of light? This is only my opinion, of course, but personally, I'm inclined to think 'C' actually stands for Christ.

How does all of this apply to our ministry? Isaiah 44:24. 26 the prophet quotes the Lord as saying,

"*...I am the LORD, ...who carries out the words of His servants and fulfills the predictions of His messengers...*"

"This is what the LORD says" . . . may be the most significant words there are.

As we walk in obedience to what the LORD says, we can expect God to work powerfully through what we say. Consider Joshua's experience in Joshua 10:12 when he led the armies of Israel against the Amorites. The battle was going their way, but they needed more time. Not one to be intimidated by mere impossibilities, Joshua asked for something that was unthinkable – for the sun and the moon to stand still in the sky until the victory was won. So on that day, the sun stood still over Gibeon, and the moon, over the Valley of Aijalon. Joshua was one of only two left alive who had seen all the miracles when God brought His people out of Egypt. His faith was full of substance.

Or how about Elijah's actions in I Kings 17: 21-22? When the son of the woman who had helped him died, he did the weirdest thing. He stretched himself out on the boy three times and cried to the LORD. He prayed that God let the boy's life return to him.!' The LORD heard Elijah's cry, and the boy's life returned to him.

Elijah had a powerful anointing on him, but his apprentice got a double anointing. Elisha could see from God's perspective and he passed on this blessing to another in II Kings 6: 16-18. His servant was terrified when he saw the armies of the enemy all around them. Elisha told him that those who were with them were more than those who were with the enemy. So Elisha asked God to give his servant spiritual sight. When the LORD opened the servant's eyes, and he looked and saw the hills full of horses and chariots of fire all around.

You might not identify with that frightened servant, but there are lots of folks who do. We must follow the example of Peter in Acts 3:6-7 as he spoke to the crippled man. He didn't have silver or gold, but he was glad to offer what he had. He freely gave out of the storehouse of God's blessing through the Spirit's power. In the name of Jesus Christ of Nazareth, he told the man to get up and walk. I love the next part. He took him by the right hand, helped him up, and instantly the man's feet and ankles became strong! Sounds like a blessing to me!

I got to thinking about Mary, the mother of Jesus and her response to Gabriel's announcement Luke 1: 38a one Christmas. When God's messenger said it, it was settled for her. She named herself the Lord's servant, and spoke her agreement. "'May it be to me as you have said. It occurs to me that this could be the very instant when Jesus was conceived in her by His Father's power and His mother's spoken release of faith.

Jesus often demonstrated His power by speaking. In Matthew 8: 25-26 the disciples went and woke him in the bottom of the boat. The storm was raging and they were terrified they going to drown. It must have been a huge storm if fishermen were terrified. He got up and rebuked the winds and the waves, telling them to be still. It became completely calm.

Or think of when he called in a loud voice to His dead friend, Lazarus, commanding him to come out in John 11: 43-44a. The man was still wrapped in the grave clothes! What amazing power!

So, what are the potentials in words? Great potential for both evil and good.

For evil:
> Hurt and devaluation.
>> Discouragement.
>>> Condemnation.
>>>> Pulling down.

For good:
> Healing.
>> Encouragement.
>>> Victory.
>>>> Lifting up.

There is a clear cause and effect in spoken words. They must be used with care, but they must be used!

Verbal Grace Gifts

Grace as unmerited favor is a concept Christians are familiar and comfortable with, but did it ever occur to you that we can use our words as verbal grace gifts?

When we verbally pass on the grace which has been handed to us, what really happens is that our mouth speaks it out of the overflow of our heart. Mathew 12:33-34 How can we help passing on the incredible abundance of blessing that has been given to us? The Holy Spirit within us causes the living water (the Word, truth of Jesus) to flow out from our hearts. John 7:38.

Not only can we bless others in response to the grace God has given us, we can bless Him. Scripture often talks about blessing the Lord. This can be done in a number of ways that not only bless Him, but bless us as well.

First, corporate worship is the way we're most accustomed to blessing the Lord.

❖ Praise verbalized by a congregation is sweet to God's ear.
❖ Music is also a powerful instrument of praise because it so powerfully includes our emotions.
❖ Prayer continues the conversation of praise, becoming more powerful as the church agrees together.

Second, we can bless Him in our devotional, quiet time. This individual worship is private and uniquely personal, but it includes many of the same elements of corporate worship.

❖ Personal spoken praise is a wonderful way to begin

❖ We can sing a new song to the Lord out of a heart filled with love and gratitude.
❖ Prayer in this setting is personal and intimate.
❖ I would also suggest you try journaling prayer.

Third, there is applied worship. This is on going, lifestyle worship. I'll never forget how reading Brother Lawrence and Frank Laubach in *Practicing the Presence*[17] impacted my thinking. The concept of practicing the presence of God changed my viewpoint. As I practiced consciously being aware of God's presence in me, I became aware of His presence all around me in my world and the lives of those around me.

Psalm 16:11 says, *"You have made known to me the path of life; you will fill me with joy in Your presence, with eternal pleasures at your right hand."*

Purpose to expand your awareness of God. How can you do to practice the presence? Let me give you a couple of ideas to get you started:

Decide to think of the Lord's presence with you every time you glance at your watch. Buy an inexpensive watch with an alarm and set it to go off periodically for a couple of days.

Charles M. Sheldon suggested in his book, In His Steps[18] at the turn of the last century that we ask ourselves what would Jesus do whenever we are faced with a decision. How about changing that to the more personal "Jesus, what would you do?"

We can also bless the Lord in our applied worship by making prayer and praise a lifestyle, not just an occasional prayer-closet activity. Do you have a worship life-style characterized by prayer and praise? If not, what can you do to improve your worship so it becomes a life-style?

Just as we desire to bless the Lord, we want to be able to receive blessing and so we can better help others do the same. So, how can we receive blessing?

We have to have sound foundations.

We have to be in right standing with God.

We need to have a right attitude about our relationship.

II Timothy 1:12b affirms that we know whom we have believed. And that we are convinced of His saving power. As Christians who are all in ministry, we understand that. What we must communicate is that like Acts 13:22 and Psalm 86: 11-12, our goal is being after God's own heart, having an undivided heart.

We need to make the decision of joy. II Corinthians concludes with a very interesting thought:

"Finally, brothers, good-by. Aim for perfection, listen to my appeal, be of one mind, live in peace. And the God of love and peace will be with you."

What makes this passage interesting is that the word is translated good-by is the Greek word 'chairo.' It was a word like the Hebrew one for peace, shalom. It was used for greeting and parting. As the Jews say 'shalom' and the Arabs, 'salaam' as a greeting even today, the first believers used the word chairo. It means 'rejoice.'

We can receive it as a choice or command, but I don't think God intended that it be optional. The world teems with grumpy Christians. What a travesty considering the presence of God in and around us.

Praise begins as a discipline, something that is learned. We are blessed when we have learned to acclaim the Lord and walk in the light of His presence. We should rejoice in His name all day long, and exalt in His righteousness. Psalm 89: 15-16 Rejoicing as a discipline.

We ourselves are lifted by being in God's presence in praise filled worship. Like I said, how can we help passing on the incredible abundance of grace that has been given to us when awareness of it's blessing floods in our minds as we praise?

Responsibility and Accountability

We need to remember that those things that come "...out of the mouth ... from the heart, are the very things that reveal our spiritual cleanliness and the degree to which we have let the Holy Spirit permeate our being. Remember, He is the one who causes the living water to flow out from our hearts into our words.

It is terribly important to take thought for what we say, both from the negative and the positive. The judgment that will be made for our reward by God will be based at least in part on our words, the things we have said. For every word, careless or otherwise, we going to be called to give account.

What we say will be tried by fire, and we'll either have cinders or crowns to lay at Jesus feet. I want to lay crowns at Jesus' feet, don't you? I can't think of anything worse than standing before God with everything I have said and done in this life piled at my feet, only to have them burst into flame under the scrutiny of God and be reduced to cinders. My desire is that there be some silver, gold, and precious jewels there when the ashes blow away.

Grace Gift Exercises

What are phrases you use when you praise the Lord? Write down at least three.

Write a blessing for the Lord using some of the words you thought of in this exercise.

Now, think of someone in your sphere of influence that you know you should bless. Think of something praiseworthy about them. Use that to write an affirmation for him or her, adding words specifically for them that would be an encouragement.

" 'For I know the plans I have for you,' declares the LORD, *'plans to prosper you and not to harm you, plans to give you* hope and a future.' "*

Jeremiah 29:11

Chapter Eight
PAINTING A VISION OF HOPE

KEY TERMS

Viewfinder
The focusing agent by which one is enabled to see clearly a desired range of vision or a specific aspect thereof as it will appear.

Envision
To see or foresee in the mind.

Christocentric
Having Christ as the center of focus or attention; having Christ as central and preeminent in importance.

KEY QUESTIONS

❖ What is the heavenly perspective?
❖ How does God view history?
❖ How should we see Jesus
❖ How do we fix our eyes?
❖ What is the foundation of our calling?
❖ How do you plant a future?
❖ How do you grow a future?
❖ How do you nurture a prizewinning crop?

From the Portals of Glory

One of the characteristics of people who are short on hope is that they look down, not up. As I thought about that, I got to wondering what the view might be like from heaven if you were able to stand on the portals of glory and look over?

What's heaven's perspective? One thing is a certainty, you'd be able to see the whole picture. II Chronicles 16:9 says that the eyes of the of the Lord move over the whole earth for an amazing purpose. It is His desire to strengthen those whose hearts are fully committed to him. His eyes are on us, ever on us, or as Job 34:21 puts it they are on the ways of men. He sees our *every* step.

Noel's favorite song is "His eye is on the Sparrow." [19] It is a wonderful reminder of God's perspective toward us., so years go I painted a scene that we having hanging over the entry way to our family room, just inside the front door with the lyrics.

His eye is on the Sparrow.

"I sing because I'm happy,
I sing because I'm free,
For His eye is on the sparrow,
And I know He watches me."

165

I love Psalm 139:7-8. Where, indeed, can I go from His Spirit? Where would it be possible to flee from His presence? If I go up to the heavens, there He is. Even if I were to make my bed in the depths of the sea, He would be there.

If we were able to peek over the portals of heaven, we'd also be able to see the whole of time – eternity– because heaven exists outside of time.

All the days of our lives are ordained for us, they were written in God's book before one of them ever comes to be. It's in the way *everlasting* that God leads us. (Psalm 139:16a, 24b)

Not only that, He says that He knows the plans He has for us. They are plans to prosper us and not to harm us, plans to give us hope and a future. (Jeremiah 29:11) This is news the people who are hurting and who have little hope desperately need to hear.

We'd be able to see people as they really are from heaven's vantage : As precious ones created in His image. No doubt we would see in something rather like double vision, and see man as fallen and sinful at the same time.

We'd see:
❖ The bondage of men, who are slaves to sin (Romans 6:17)
❖ That they are blind and deceived.

"And even if our gospel is veiled, it is veiled to those who are perishing. The god of this age has blinded the minds of unbelievers, so that they cannot see the light of the gospel of the glory of Christ, who is the image of God."
II Corinthians 4:3-4

❖ That they are hurting, that they're lost, like sheep that have gone astray (Isaiah 53:6a)

❖ That they're dying , because the wages that are earned for sin is death. Romans 6:23a

You'd also see that from the divine viewpoint, they are redeemable and savable because everyone who calls on the name of the Lord will be saved. (Acts 2:21)

God's has a view of history that is beyond what we can see, but it's definitely a head's up view, not head down. History really is His story. It tells of His relationship with men, like:

Abraham, God's friend;
David, a man after God's own heart. ;
With sons and heirs, for whom He becomes a father.

History relates the story of covenant that He made with men, a covenant He considers an obligation which is irrevocable. He declares of Himself,

"I am the Lord; I change not."

His story of is told in the law and the prophets, through which He reveals His instructions, His standard. They are a merciful gift to men so sin could be identified and dealt with. The standard also contains the opportunity to be accepted by Him.

His story tells of redemption and restoration. There was the immediate provision after the fall, but also the ongoing forgiveness that He made available.

His story has a blueprint:

For creation.

For man.

God's perspective is an overview. *But*, it's not heaven yet! Neither is it as far off as we might be inclined to think. We need to do our best to keep eternity in view.

As long as we're considering some perspective shifts, what about how we view Jesus?

Having a Jesus Fixation

How should we see Jesus? He has got to be central because everything revolves around His person. The church is built on and revolves around Christ. We have a Christocentric church.

Every facet of the faith reflects Christ ~ the Christocentric faith. As believers, Christ is at the core of who and what we are ~ the Christocentric believer.

How do we fix our eyes? Let's consider Hebrews 12:1-2a

"Therefore, since we are surrounded by such a great cloud of witnesses, let us throw off everything that hinders and the sin that so easily entangles, and let us run with perseverance the race marked out for us. Let us fix our eyes on Jesus, the author and perfecter of our faith..."

We fix our eyes by paying attention to our testimony, what we have to share about our first hand experiences with God. There is a great cloud of witnesses comprised of those who've gone before us who are watching and cheering us on.

❖ *Throw off* everything that hinders, everything that gets in the way of seeing Jesus and following after him. Throw it off!

❖ *Run the* race with perseverance. Amble and stroll aren't in the text. Running implies vigorous, focused, disciplined movement.

❖ *Wholly, steadfastly* look to Jesus. Our whole attention, without wavering. A quick glance won't be sufficient. We must consider these things, meditate and reflect. We are a people who have been called by God.

What's the foundation of our calling? To make Jesus central in our life of faith. We aren't primarily people who are called to do; *He's called us to be.* Our foundation is Christ in us, the hope of glory. This relationship is the true source of our hope. All the things that God wants to do through us are accomplished through our obedience and our relationship, not our effort. *What I do naturally flows out of who I am.*

How can we focus on being?

❖ Abiding in Christ We're branches, not the vine. God doesn't call you to leadership as the first step; it is an outgrowth of your life in Christ. Helping others see that they aren't first called to do, they're called to be has got to be one of our highest priorities.

❖ Practicing the presence.   Consider how you can make yourself more conscious of God's presence with you. In chapter six I suggested setting a watch alarm to go off periodically for a couple of days. You might set aside a time each day to meditate.   Purpose to notice His handiwork. It will take some effort, but it is well worth it.

❖ Putting on the mind of Christ. When we succeed in allowing Christ to permeate and direct our thoughts, we end up with two wills operating as one. We aren't on the hook for delivering hope to people, because Christ does it.

Here is an exercise to help you think this through. Write a brief summary of who you are in Christ. When you've finished, formulate a short list of steps (involving attitude or action) that can be taken to help us see a person as God sees them.

Seed Planting

How do we plant a future? By planting truth. God's truth gives us hope.

Luke 8:5 tells the parable of the farmer who went out to sow his seed. What we come to see in the parable is that the seed is the Word. Luke 8:11

Saying just any old thing in an attempt to encourage someone and give them hope doesn't work; in no time at all you'll find yourself giving out pabulum (i.e. baby food) and lies. It has to be truth based in the Word.

God has specific truth for individual people at particular times. If we pray and ask, He'll reveal what that is.

In the central San Joaquin Valley of California we understand that planting is part of a process which doesn't produce a crop for harvest overnight. Dr. George O. Wood, General Secretary of the Assemblies of God, applied this concept to the work of missions in his sermon, "Three Laws of Harvest," but it applies equally well to planting a future through blessing. A harvest cannot be reaped which hasn't been sewn, but neither can it be reaped until it has grown. We may not see the results of the future we sow. It isn't always part of God's plan that we see both the beginning and the end of the work He does through us.

Let me give you a suggestion for seed planting in your own home, because it is unconscionable that we would bless others, and not bless our own.. Many years ago we wrote out the Daniels' Family Goals. We shared them with our children, then Noel thumb-tacked them on the inside of the

171

cupboard where we store the dinner plates. Each day when the kids set the table, there they were. They set out what we hoped for, what we wanted to work toward: for us as parents, for them as children, and for them as people who were growing into Christian adults. The sheet is now slightly yellowed with age, but it still hangs there for Benjamin, our youngest, and the next generation.

GOALS OF THE DANIELS' FAMILY

1. Solve the big problems:
   How do we perceive life and death?
   What principles will we live by?
   The Bible is the source for answers.
2. Learn to rely on God as our source.
3. Know who we are fighting and whose side we are on (this was a reference to Satan and God.)
4. Give ourselves away through service.
5. Choose the positive: be part of the solution.
6. Write out your situation: Goals, needs blessings, options, budgets, etc. Think and talk with yourself and the family. Allow the Spirit to work. T – bar analysis.
7. Build events into our lives and record them for remembering.
8. Look around and note what you see. Be observant. Respond to what is there.
9. Learn to fail and rise.
10. Stay in prayer, communing with God. Pray in concern for others.
11. Pray for the person you're going to marry or are married to.
12. Always tell the truth.

Other short range goals for your children can also be a terrific tool for helping them visualize their personal future and have steadfast hope in it. These can be posted on the wall in the child's room or on the refrigerator. They might include things like the daily tasks which are their responsibility for which they will be rewarded. This can be anything from bed making and household chores to homework or Sunday school assignments.

Don't forget the importance of reading the Word in your home, especially to the children when they're small. Ben wouldn't go to sleep when he was little without his Bible story. We have often read the Word when we were away from home on vacation and were not able to attend a church.

Once we plant the seeds of truth, how do we grow a future?

By modeling and teaching obedience:
To the Word,
To the Holy Spirit,
To those in authority.

Modeling and teaching obedience act as keys
To hope,
To peace,
To effectiveness

Faith and trust are illustrated thereby as two sides of the same coin. We believer God and take Him at His Word, then we trust Him to do for us what is best. A lot of us are better at believing than we are at trusting!

So, how do we nurture a prizewinning crop? Nothing will do but our utmost for His highest. In that process, we need to be looking for the potential God sees:

In ourselves

In others

Strive for excellence versus being satisfied with the passable or acceptable. The world strives for excellence, often in things that are of absolutely no consequence. Surely we can do no less.

What phrases or verses can you think of which picture a hope and a future that would be lifting words?

Using one of the phrases or verses you thought of, write words that paint a vision of hope and a future for the one you thought of in the last exercise.

*"My command
is this:
Love each other
as I have love you.
Greater love
has no one than this,
that he
lay down his life
for his friends."*

John 15:12

Chapter Nine
PARTNERING FOR FOLLOW-THROUGH

KEY TERMS

Compassion
A feeling of involvement in the suffering of another which prompts a desire to help or spare.

Encouragement
The giving of courage, hope, confidence or resolution.

Acceptance
The act of receiving with favor, with willingness, as satisfactory and approved.

Communion
A mutual sharing of thoughts, feelings or participation; fellowship.

KEY QUESTIONS

- ❖ What is the foundation for the bonds of Christian love?
- ❖ What are eyes of compassion?
- ❖ What is a servant's heart?
- ❖ How can we have wings of love?
- ❖ What ties bind us?
- ❖ What results from acceptance?
- ❖ What does liberation produce?

The Bonds of Love

The bonds of love truly are the ties that bind our hearts together in Christian love, as the old hymn says:[20]

Blest be the tie that binds
Our hearts in Christian love;
The fellowship of kindred minds
Is like to that above.

Have you ever had the experience of meeting another believer somewhere, striking up a conversation, and discovering that it feels like you have known him a long time? Or have you ever been in a secular group, perhaps a business function, and found you gravitated to the Christians during a social hour without knowing in advance who they were? The Spirit of God in us recognizes that same Spirit in the lives of others.

Christian love binds us because of the very nature of God and His love. Jeremiah 31: 3 has always been one of my favorite verses. He loves you and me with an *everlasting* love; because of it He has drawn us to Himself and to each other with lovingkindness. It is the nature of our relationship to God in love that ties us to Him. He is our *'Abba, Father.'* (Romans 8: 15) We are a people belonging to God (I Peter 2:9a.)

The nature of our relationship to Christ ties us as well, because we are heirs with Him. He was the only son of

179

the Father, but like Ephraim and Manasseh we have been adopted and now share in the double blessing that came to Jesus. We have become heirs of God and co – heirs with Christ. (Romans 8:17)

And finally, we're bound by the nature of our relationship to each other. Jesus' command to us is this: Love each other as I have loved you. There is no greater love than this, that we love each other so much that we would even be willing to lay down our life for our friends. (John 15:12-13)

The result of the acceptance of the ties that bind us are:

❖ Fellowship ~ rich, full, warm, loving fellowship. And
❖ Unity. We're one in the bonds of love. One body, with one head, whose hearts beat as one.

How incredible it is that bonds of love are so liberating, opening the doors of sin's prison. What a contrast to the bonds of sin. They are heavy chains that confine in a prison without walls as surely as any penitentiary.

The liberation that comes with knowing Jesus is exhilarating and dynamic. The chains that kept us bound in misery are loosened. The things that bind us and so easily entangle fall off and we are free. We talked earlier about throwing those things off in the Hebrews 12:1 passage. I saw a poster recently that showed ankles suddenly released from shackles to run free. There is running and dancing and celebrating when a prisoner is set free.

So many people that come across our paths, perhaps even some of us, cling to what scripture refers to as the familiarity of Egypt. Remember when the children of Israel had barely arrived in the desert, and they began to clamor for the supposed luxuries they had left behind? How soon we forget how awful a price sin has extracted in our lives! Why would we ever chose the very thing that we wanted desperately to be free of? I can't imagine going back into slavery for vegetables! The familiarity of Egypt is our old misery inducing sin, but the thing is, it's known and understood. We may not like it, but it's familiar, and oddly comfortable.

People hang on to the past when they don't have real confidence in the future because:

They've never heard or
They haven't been able to envision it.

We can do that for them. We need to understand that it's a *critical* part of our job.

This brings up another wonderful result of being liberated: communion. As we bless people, the block of hopelessness begins to fall and fellowship can become a reality. The walls that not only confined but separated come tumbling down, and connection is made. Even more exciting, they can begin to enter into real partnership with us in the faith.

Following Christ's Example

Each of the steps of blessing were integral parts of what Jesus consistently did during His three years of earthly ministry. He modeled for us what He wants us to do as well as how He wants us to do it. The Gospels illustrate time and again that:

❖ Jesus went out of His way to touch people.
❖ His words and actions demonstrated the high value He put each person.
❖ His language was powerful.
❖ He brought God's perspective through His life, death and resurrection, opening wide the doorway of hope and guarantying our future
❖ He demonstrated His commitment to us by sending the Holy Spirit and promising to come again. He said:

"I tell you the truth, anyone who has faith in me will do what I have been doing. He will do even greater things than these, because I am going to the Father." John 14:12

When we give a biblical blessing we're following in Jesus' footsteps, acting according to the precedent He set, and following his example. What's really happening is we are doing His work His way. We're majoring on the majors! It guarantees we'll have eyes to see things His way, that we will have eyes of compassion.

The supernatural is the genuine, original natural. God's way is true reality, not the stunted, twisted reality sin perceives. Choosing to take heaven's viewpoint is keeping eternity in the frame of our viewfinder.

As we make this conscious choice of seeing from God's perspective, how logical a result it is that having our eyes fixed on the goal becomes not only possible for us, it becomes easy and natural.

Travis was in a class I was teaching recently, and he told me how he had learned to make it up difficult hills while out jogging. He struggled with this particular challenge until a running friend gave him a fascinating technique. He looked at the top of the hill, his goal, and envisioned a long rope extended from that point down to him at the bottom of the hill. Once he grabbed onto the rope, he imagined he was pulling hand over hand up its length. The interesting result was that it helped him keep his eye on where he was going, and gave him the psychological boost of strength he needed to make it. Jesus offers us a lifeline up the hills of challenge He sets before us on our way to the goal where He is standing in plain sight for us. But the most wonderful part of all is we don't have to do all the pulling and running! He pulls on His end by the Holy Spirit, helping us all along the way. As long as we hold on, keep looking up at Him, keep our eyes *fixed* on Him, the hills are made low and the race is won.

Having God's perspective also means we'll have farmer's eyes that see fields white unto harvest. (John 4:35) Harvesting isn't the only work God allows us to do with Him. As farmers in His field, there have many tasks that God is busily going about in which He allows us to join Him. We can join Him in

Cultivating the soil of lives that need something from Him through the preparation of blessing.
Planting the Word in language the Spirit directs that is chosen just for them.

183

Watering with prayer as an expression for our
partnering for support.
Nurturing the crop by teaching, mentoring, and
leading.
Weeding carefully by gently correcting when the
Spirit prompts.
Harvesting. Not just bringing into the kingdom, but to
maturity, full bloom.

One word of caution: Don't fall into the trap of feeling sorry for people. We need empathy so that we can adequately understand and feel *with them*. However, sympathy is something else entirely. It means taking their side, which may not be the side Jesus is on. Jesus is *for us*, as Don Moen's musical work so beautifully describes, but He is not *for our sin*. Often, sympathy is something that is too closely akin to enabling.

What we must strive for is a servant's heart. This means we operate in Christ's love in Christ's way. We're not called to be robots or mindless slaves. We must be stewards who are responsible, adopted family members, striving to bring the people He brings into our sphere of influence to the same place.

As we operate in Christ's love, God increases the capacity of *our* love. What God develops in us is *wings of love*. Like the hen who offers protection for the young under her wings:

From the enemy.
From the old life.
From themselves and their fallen nature.

We're given the incredible opportunity of participating in the training and encouragement of those under our ministry: We're hens whose goal is to give flying lessons to the fledgling chicks. We do that by

Blessing
Affirming
Nurturing
Modeling
Mentoring
Partnering

We need to help these dear ones plug into the programs which are available through our churches that will aid us in the process. We aren't in this endeavor alone. We are part of the Body, working together.

Ultimately, we'll offer soloing trust to the fledglings we have blessed and loved, nurtured and encouraged. As a church, we'll trust them with responsibility and leadership.

As I was finishing this work, I received an unsolicited but *very worth reading* letter in the mail. It carried the banner heading GOOD NEWS. Naturally I thought it was from a Christian ministry of some sort. Not even close!

It was from a psychic who is selling "psychic /astrological readings!" Listen to the terminology she uses:

Why is she sending this letter to me? "Simply because, in my heart, I know that you feel lost, and I want to bring you home." (She's addressing the "lonely and isolated" need.)

She says, "You are a giving person ... very intelligent, sensitive..." and other very flattering things. (Affirmation)

"You are the most important person in the world, and your future and your personal well-being are what I care most about right now!   …An incredible, huge sum of money may be in your future." (Personal language just for me, painting a vision of a hopeful future in which she will partner with me and support me.)

The topper was this: "Every day I hold a prayer vigil for my special clients. When you write back to me I will give you a special phone number for you to call, so that I can include your prayers for money, health, love, family, or whatever it is in life you wish for are included too!"

People desperately need blessing. Someone not in God's plan may step in to fill that need if we don't!

To wrap up, I'd like you to do some something. Identify people with whom you need to partner by category. Your categories may include spouse, children grandchildren, parents, siblings or other family members. How about the people in authority over you in the family of God, as well as those who are under you? Include acquaintances, and so on.

List your categories by *priority*. Identify the *type* of partnering needed in each case: i.e. parenting, teaching, modeling, supporting, etc.

Write a *short* partnering statement for each, like: I will faithfully teach, or I will pray.

Person	Type of Partnering	Partnering Statement

Write a blessing for two of them:
Check your blessing for the five steps.

1.

2.

"The LORD
bless you and keep you;
the LORD
make his face shine upon
you
and be gracious to you;
the LORD
turn his face toward you
and give you peace.
they will put my name
on the Israelites,
and I will bless them."

Numbers 6:24-27

Chapter Ten
FORMULATING BLESSINGS

As you begin to put into practice what you've been learning, relax and enjoy yourself! Blessing is something that brings *you* great joy, not just the person you're lifting through blessing. Remember that the more parts of the biblical paradigm you use, the more powerful the blessing will be. Besides the day to day opportunities, give thought to special occasions where you can plan for a blessing. Wedding rehearsal dinners, wedding receptions (perhaps instead of the toast), baby/wedding showers, birthdays, anniversaries, retirement parties, and graduations are just a few of the times where a blessing would be wonderful. They can be written down and framed as gifts, as well.

Here are some informal examples. Notice the 5 steps.

Placing his **hands** (1) on his son's shoulders, the father says: (2) "**Josh**, you're the Lord's gift to Mom and me. (3) **You are** growing strong in body, mind and spirit. (4) The Lord is **leading you** in the way you should go; **He'll complete** the good work He has begun in you, and He'll do great things through you as you follow Him. As you run the race that is set before you, may your eyes be fixed on the prize of the high calling that the Lord has for you in Christ Jesus. (5) **We'll always** be on the sidelines to cheer you on and help you."

(1) Picking up his little girl in the garden and **hugging** her, the daddy says, (2) "**Chrissie**, you're Daddy's little lily. You make me smile all over!" Tickling her under the chin he

191

adds, (3) "You know what? Jesus **is growing you** into a beautiful person, just like those flowers. (4) **He'll always give** you everything you need, just like the lilies in the field. What you do will be like the sweet smell of these flowers, pleasing to the Lord because you'll grow as you feed on His Word and are watered by the Holy Spirit. (5) And you know what? He's letting me be assistant gardener to **help you grow!**"

(1) Taking the **hand** of her friend, the woman says, (2) "**Sue** you are so genuine in your faith, deeply rooted, like a tree God has planted by a river. (3) I see people come to you to rest in your shadow for a while when they're tired and **you help them.** God is your strength and you generously share it. (4) He is growing fruit on your branches. **I see love,** joy, peace, patience, kindness. They're all there: goodness, faithfulness, gentleness and self-control. Your graciousness will influence many for God. (5) You are an important part of **my team** in the women's ministry in our church."

1) Walking **arm in arm** with her husband, the wife says, (2) **Noel,** did I ever tell you how much I admire the way you head our family in spiritual things? (3) **You have such** a gentle way of leading, not bossy or unreasonable so it's easy for me to follow you. I know that you ask the Lord to lead you, and you care about me, what I think and feel. I can see how you love me, like Jesus loves the church. (4) **Our children won't stray** from the Lord, because you're training them in the way they should go. I know you will continue to grow in wisdom, and standing in the community, and that you will have favor with people and the Lord. The Lord will prosper everything you do because you seek Him. (5) I'm glad I get to be **your helpmate!**"

Chapter Eleven
FOOD FOR THOUGHT

Questions for personal consideration or discussion in a Bible study setting. The scriptures for each of these questions can be found in the text.

1. Define biblical blessing.

2. Explain the steps of the biblical blessing.

3. What is the context for giving a blessing in scripture?

4. List 5 reasons people need to be blessed.

5. Name three ways that Jehovah is unique.

7. How does God reach out to man?

8. How does touch affect people?

9. What do eyes of love see?

10. How is God's perspective different from man's?

11. What ways can you affirm someone?

12. Contrast God's valuation and man's for worth, strength, and wisdom.

13. What difference could a shift in one's attitude paradigm make in ministry?

14. How does God activate his will?

15. What are the potentials in words?

16. What can help us receive blessing?

17. What especially strikes you as important in Matthew 12:33-37 regarding responsibility and accountability?

18. What are some aspects of heaven's perspective that could effect man's perspective:

19. How does God's view of history differ from man's?

20. How should we see Jesus?

21. What's the foundation of our calling?

22. How do we plant a future for someone? What are some of your own ideas?

23. Which element of growing a future seems the most challenging to you?

24. How do we nurture a prizewinning crop?

25. What ties bind us?

26. What results from acceptance?

27. How important are the results of liberation?

28. What's the difference between empathy and sympathy?

29. What difference would having a servant's heart make?

30. How can a blessing encourage and lift someone?

Notes

Introduction

1. *The Real Mother Goose,* Rand McNally & Company, Chicago, 1916, 1971 edition, p. 101.

Chapter One – BLOCKS TO BLESSING

2. Gary Smalley and John Trent, Ph.D., *The Blessing,* Simon and Schuster Inc., New York, NY, 1986.
3. People Magazine, Special Collector's Edition, *The Most Intriguing People of the Century,* 1998.
4. Kenneth Turan, Los Angeles Times film critic. Valley Public Radio, *Morning Edition,* Friday, February 2, 2002.
5. Henry Blackaby, *Experiencing God,* Lifeway Press, Nashville, TN, 1990.
6. *What Women Want,* Nancy Meyers, with Mel Gibson, Helen Hunt, and Marissa Tomai. Paramount, 2001.

Chapter Three – THE NEED FOR BLESSING

7. Sharon Moshavi, Valley Public Radio, *Morning Edition,* Tuesday, February 26, 2002
8. Ralph Ellison, *The Invisible Man,* Vintage Press, New York, 1949, 1995
9. John Donne, *No Man is an Island,* Louis Untermeyer, Compiler, *A Treasury of Great Poems,* Simon and Schuster, New York, NY, 1955, p. 355-356.

Chapter Four - THE LIFTING TOUCH

10. Anna B. Warner, lyricist, "Jesus Loves Me," 1820 – 1915, William B. Bradbury, composer, 1816-1868
11. Matthew Henry, *Matthew Henry's Commentary* (Concise), WORDsearch 4 Discipleship Library, NavPress Software, s 1987-1996.
12. Bill and Gloria Gaither, "His Love Reaching," *His Love Reaching*, Paragon Music, 1975.
13. Annie Johnson Flint, lyricist, "He Giveth More Grace," 1941. Renewed 1969 by Lillenas Publishing Co. p. 415

Chapter Five - LIFTING VALUE

14. Darlene Zscheh, "Worthy is the Lamb," Hillsong Publishing, 2000
15. Charles H. Gabriel, "He Lifted Me," *The Hymnal for Worship & Celebration,* Word Music, Waco, TX, 1986, p. 522
16. D. James Kennedy, Ph.D., *Evangelism Explosion*, Tyndale House Publishing, Inc., Wheaton, IL, 1996

Chapter Six - LIFTING LANGUAGE

17. Gene Edwards, editor, Brother Lawrence and Frank Laubach, *Practicing His Presence,* The Seed Sowers, Beaumont, TX, 1973
18. Charles M. Sheldon, 1857-1946, *In His Steps,* 1896, Republished Barbour Publishing, Inc., 1997

19. Civilla D. Martin, "His Eye is on the Sparrow," Public Domain, *The Celebration Hymnal,* Word/Integrity, Inc., USA, 1998, p. 624

20. John Fawcett, "Blest Be the Tie That Binds," *The Hymnal for Worship & Celebration,* Word Music, Waco, TX, 1986 p. 286